ALL TYPES OF CONFLICT CAN BE RESOLVED

HEZEKIAH BROWN

Printed in the United States of America

Library of Congress Control Number: 2020919851
ISBN: Softcover   978-1-64908-435-4
           eBook   978-1-64908-434-7
           Hardback   978-1-64908-522-1

Republished by: PageTurner Press and Media LLC
Publication Date: 11/24/2020

To order copies of this book, contact:
PageTurner Press and Media
Phone: 1-888-447-9651
order@pageturner.us
www.pageturner.us

ALL TYPES OF CONFLICT CAN BE RESOLVED

CONTENTS

Foreword

In late 1979, I was working as an assistant to the president of the United Federation of Teachers, which is the largest local in the American Federation of Teachers. At the time, I had never served as a chief spokesman during collective bargaining. Despite that, I received a daunting assignment from Albert Shanker, the AFT president: negotiate a collective bargaining agreement for the teachers at the United Nations International School, which had secretly affiliated with the AFT because the teachers feared the reaction of the Soviet Union, which was hostile to the American labor because it was avowedly anti-communist.

The teachers had been working without a contract for more than a year. In addition, many of the teachers were foreign nationals who had green cards, which might be forfeit were they out of work due to a strike.

Many of these same teachers were willing to strike despite their vulnerability. Consequently, I was precluded by Mr. Shanker from permitting the teachers to strike. Faced with this conundrum and given my relative inexperience, I was in desperate need of a guide. Fortunately, upon arriving at my initial bargaining session, I found that an astute federal mediator had been assigned to the dispute in the person of Hezekiah Brown, with whom I was unacquainted.

In encountering Hez, I found an enthusiastic leader who projected confidence that he would enable us to peacefully conclude a fair contract. He recognized the volatile nature of the bargaining unit's leadership and the dangers they presented to themselves, and he empowered me to convince them to accept a rational, common-sense compromise—no easy task given the situation.

Hez's approach to mediation and negotiation is rooted in his comfort with conflict. In his view, conflict is not something to be feared or suppressed. Rather, conflict is an opportunity to learn and grow if properly managed.

So how did Hezekiah Brown acquire the skills and develop his approach to conflict resolution?

Hez was raised in the Jim Crow South by his mother and oldest sister with eight siblings. His values were forged in a church-centered community. After entering the service, he was selected as one of the first African Americans for airborne school at Fort Campbell, Kentucky, where he had to endure racial taunting. After successfully graduating, Hez was deployed to Little Rock in 1956 when President Eisenhower enforced a federal court order to integrate the schools there.

Ultimately, Hez emigrated from the South to Buffalo, New York, where his sister had moved. He obtained employment in a steel plant and was quickly chosen by his coworkers to serve as a shop steward and then local president. When the Federal Mediation and Conciliation Service (FMCS) initiated a program to recruit new mediators with labor experience, Hez was chosen.

After serving as a federal mediator, Hez worked as director for the Cornell University School of Industrial Labor Relations Extension Program in New York City, training labor and management advocates in dispute resolution skills; was appointed chair of the New York

State Employment Relations Board by Governor Mario Cuomo; was elected to the Board of Education School Board in Hempstead, New York; and was deputy county executive of Nassau County.

With his son, Rodney, Mr. Brown also operated a firm that trained youth in how to peacefully resolve conflicts with others. Some of the youth included young men who had experienced legal problems. Mr. Brown has successfully applied the skills of grievance processing and collective bargaining to problems encountered in everyday life.

This book is an extremely useful guide on how to employ conflict resolution skills in daily life situations. I am confident that the reader who pursues the lessons of this book will experience growth and self-actualization. The reader will enjoy the satisfaction that comes with the skill set necessary to resolve interpersonal problems.

David Stein
Arbitrator/Mediator

About the Author

HEZEKIAH BROWN
Arbitrator-Mediator
Consultant

In 2003, Hezekiah Brown retired from his position as deputy county executive and moved to Elizabeth City, North Carolina. He currently serves as a member of the Board of Visitors at Elizabeth City State University and the Elizabeth City–Pasquotank County Planning and Library Board; vice chair of the Hope Group; and former member of the Elizabeth City–Pasquotank County Community Relations Commission.

Hezekiah has had a long and successful career as a professional neutral. He has mediated and arbitrated over five thousand labor-management, community, and a wide range of other types of disputes. In 1972, he was selected to serve as a federal mediator. He served with honors for twelve years as a commissioner with the Federal Mediation and Conciliation Service and mediated some of the most difficult disputes. These included disputes between the New York League of Voluntarily Hospital and 1199SEIU United Health Care Workers Union that covered an excess of one hundred thousand employees, Consolidated Edison for fourteen thousand employees, United Parcel Service, International Brotherhood of

Teamsters for four thousand employees, Group Health Insurance, Office of Professional Employees International Union, Bridgeport University, Adelphi University, Wagner College, Bernard College, United Nations School, Rochester School District, and thousands of other significant community disputes, including personal relation and business. He has worked as a professional neutral, teacher, and trainer facilitator for over forty-five years.

His other expertise includes joint labor-management resolution, employment discrimination, and resolving community, business, and relationship disputes.

In 1985, he was recruited by Cornell University's extension in New York City to join the staff at the Director of Labor-Management programs. His responsibility was to teach credit and noncredit courses, including anger management, problem-solving, managing conflict, arbitration, mediation, team building, change management, contract administration, and diversity. In addition, he was responsible for implementing numerous successful nontraditional joint labor-management initiatives with large companies in New York, New Jersey, Maine, Connecticut, Pennsylvania, and Michigan.

Additionally, he and Ouida Vendryes wrote the curriculum for the Cornell University Extension five-day Dispute Resolution Certificate Program, which attracted students from the United States, Saudi Arabia, Bangladesh, Cypress, Italy, South America, and Australia.

In 1992, he was selected as one of ten instructors to visit Russia to teach contract administration and conflict resolution as they embarked on making the transition to a market economy.

In 1995, he was again selected as one of ten instructors to travel to Europe to study the global application of cooperation between labor and management.

Upon his return from Europe, he was selected by the United States secretary of labor Robert Reich to serve on the Labor-Management Task Force on Excellence in State and Local Government. This was a two-year assignment where the task force traveled throughout the country examining innovative and productive Labor-Management projects that could be replicated in other institutions. After the task force work, it was unanimously accepted by the United States Congress.

In 1999, Hezekiah retired from Cornell University Extension and started a family-owned and family-operated business—Brown, Brown & Associates Conflict Resolution Training Center—and quickly gained notoriety as one of the most diversified and competent companies in dispute resolution in the state of New York. Their largest clients were the health care and utility industries.

Hezekiah received a bachelor of science degree from the State University of New York, Empire State College, and was awarded an honorary PhD from Cornell University Extension.

In 2008, he was inducted into the Prestigious National Academy of Arbitrators in Ottawa, Canada.

In 1957, while serving as a US Army paratrooper in 101st Airborne Division (327 Airborne Battle Group), Specialist Brown was deployed to Little Rock, Arkansas, to help enforce the desegregation of Little Rock Central High School.

He has been married to Zelma Christine for fifty-seven years. They are the proud parents of Rodney and Chandra, and grandparents to one granddaughter, Crystal.

Introduction

From migrant farmworker and high school dropout to some
of the most powerful and important positions in the United
States—president of a Union, federal mediator, New York
State chief mediator, commissioner, arbitrator, deputy county
executive of Nassau, community advocate, member of the
National Academy of Arbitrators, entrepreneur, and politician

I traveled this journey from migrant farmworker and high school
dropout to some of the most powerful positions in the United
States. I, along with many others, am still trying to figure
out how I skillfully navigated this sophisticated and complicated
system without compromising any of my core values of hard work,
honesty, and respect for others to such a high degree of acceptance,
coming from a poverty-stricken neighborhood and being poor
and uneducated.

I came from what society has labeled as a broken family. While
we had some difficult days, through it all, we survived and became
stronger and closer through love and supporting from each other.
The Brown family was never broken. While it was unfortunate
that my mother and father separated after having eleven children,
we weathered the storm. Incidentally, our father disappeared for
twenty-five years, and we had absolutely no contact with him
during his absence. After our father left, we as a family of sisters and

brothers, along with a devoted mother, became strong supporters and champions for one another. We did not let society's label (broken family) affect us. In fact, we became closer, more protective, and more supportive of each other.

I finally figured it out. It was only by the grace of God. He gave me a loving and devoted wife, Zelma Christine, the mother of our children Rodney and Chandra. I also have an exemplary supportive family—Doris, Roberta, Margaret, (deceased) Theresa, Willie, Ann, Cozy, Paula, Nathaniel, Ann, Johnnie (deceased), Sammie, David Tommie, Bettie—and numerous extended family members—Dorothy, Willie Elma, Tyrone and Irene, and two special friends and mentors, Gary and Sharon Griggs.

My family was, and continues to be, extremely proud of me and the things that I have accomplished by navigating this complicated system to reach some of the top and most powerful positions in the country. There are others in this wonderful family who also took advantage of what is offered in this great country. Some family members became successful authors, educators, managers, supervisors, and entrepreneurs. We continue to stay close as a family, with the same spirit of love, respect, and support for each other. We all continue to believe that we are a blessed family, showing appreciation through God and sharing our talents and blessings with the communities throughout the United States. "To God be the glory for all the things He has done."

Peacemaker, Teacher, Trainer

We're all different. We look different. We believe different things. We respond differently to situations. We want different results. Therefore, while our differences are things that make us unique when we're faced with opposing ideas, beliefs, and structures, our differences cause conflict. Sometimes these conflicts create intense verbal debates; one side is arguing to prove their ideas are better than the other side. And sometimes these conflicts cause such rifts that neither side wins and the matter goes unresolved. Conflicts have a strange way of allowing people to voice their opposing opinions and discover a way to compromise. Conflicts also have a strange way of creating so much animosity and tension. It seems easier to walk away with your beliefs intact instead of jeopardizing everything else.

I've spent years listening to people come together to argue their sides and draw up a resolution. My professions and what I've come to recognize as my God-given talent are dispute resolution and negotiation. I have made a living from teaching people how to sit down, reluctantly sometimes, and voice their version of the story while also listening to the other party's version of the story. In some cases, both parties have realized that their disputes are frivolous or have no foundation to stand on. And in some cases, there's no denying that there's a serious issue at hand that absolutely must be resolved—and soon.

While I'd like to think of myself as a peacemaker, that's far from the technical skill and knowledge that is necessary to solve a dispute or negotiate a balanced resolution. It takes a special skill for listening, speaking, thinking, and investigating to perform the job that I hold near and dear to my heart. You would probably like to think that most people should naturally have the skill for listening, speaking, thinking, and investigating. After all, we are born with two ears, a mouth, and a brain, and that is half of the battle. However, in times of dispute and conflict, while we are born with the right tools (ears, a mouth, and a brain), most people don't always use them, and they certainly don't use them properly.

Think about it: The last time you were in a conflict where your opinions, beliefs, and ideas opposed another person's, did you take the time to effectively listen to them, rebut with facts and findings, think before you speak, or otherwise approach the situation willing to compromise? If you did, then you are an impeccable communicator who can diffuse situations before they have a chance to develop. However, if you are one of the many who are headstrong on their opinion and really want to "win" in a dispute, then in most cases, you have probably voluntarily avoided listening, speaking, thinking, and investigating. After all, who has time for all that when the main focus is to *win*!

What Do I Know about Solving Problems?

My profession has taken me to multiple countries, and I have worked in multiple industries. Whether it was education, politics, government, or labor relations, there was always a dispute. The blue-collar employees would want something better than what the white collars were offering. One political party blamed the other for the grievances of a city, state, or region. Teachers wanted something different than the administrators were willing to give. No matter what, the issue was always a tug-of-war between opposing parties who shared the same physical and occupational spaces. Sure, they worked together for the common agenda, but that was the end of their similarities. Everything else was disputable, from pay to schedules and benefits to rights or privileges. They could agree on the common goal of getting the job done, but they could not agree on the methods, strategies, background arrangements, or anything else that made it conducive for both parties to do their part and actually do the work.

This has been my primary focus for years—seeing to it that people understand each other's viewpoints. They begin to find common ground, compromise, and establish a working relationship. Both parties can become satisfied. Sometimes my work takes just a few hours. Sometimes I deal with the back-and-forth disputing for months. Either way, I've never walked away from the table with a situation that has been closed as "unresolved." Why? Because I clearly understand the fundamentals of dispute resolution, negotiation, and bringing disputants together. I have never forsaken those principles, regardless of the occupation, industry, or area in which I've worked.

I've seen tremendous success in executing the art of dispute resolution and negotiation. I've received the plaques, accolades, and news clippings to prove it. However, I've learned that there's a bigger picture besides resolving conflicts for others. The bigger picture is that I must use my skill to teach people how to resolve conflicts for themselves.

One of the main miscommunication issues comes from the fact that we don't teach people how to resolve conflicts. In fact, we actually teach them how to create them. Society is very much the blame for many of the day-to-day disputes that arise between people. The subliminal messages we receive, the jealousy over materialistic things, the ability to avoid having meaningful conversations, the ability to spread misinformation at the speed of lightning without being held accountable for the fallacies, the ability to text what we feel and think instead of sitting down face-to-face to express ourselves—all of these things contribute to our inability to solve problems. Why? Because society has made it very easy and very acceptable to sweep things under the rug and avoid the tough conversations.

Why Are We Arguing in the First Place?

When we begin to rationalize why disputes exist, we can learn that disputes don't exist due to differences in personality. They exist because of our behaviors. Our behaviors dictate our responses to the situations we find ourselves in. When we respond to a dispute with negative behaviors such as animosity, pigheadedness, anger, or greed, these disputes become very difficult to solve.

Disputes start and become harder to resolve because, in general, people bring a lot of emotional and mental baggage to the table. Although we'd like to think that we're arguing about one subject, the baggage we bring into these arguments fuels the fire for us to argue with such passion and indignant attitudes that sometimes we forget why we're arguing in the first place.

In my years of sitting at a table, in the middle of two opposing parties I've realized that neither side chooses to acknowledge the other side's turmoil. No one knows what the other person or group of people are dealing with. There's no sense of compassion or understanding. Yes, it's a bit more difficult to do in a professional setting. However, humanity trumps professional settings. Common respect trumps all disputes. There's an idiom that says "In order to get respect, you've got to give respect." For this to be the case, we have to learn to tame the beast that dictates how much respect we give and receive and that ultimately determines how far a dispute will go—the ego.

While I am the professional neutral at one end of the table, willing to mediate/negotiate and use every tool in my professional arsenal to settle a dispute. Two very large egos are also at the table, unwilling to loosen their grips. Egos build tremendous momentum for disputes, allowing them to grow. It becomes more dangerous and impactful and goes without resolution for however long it takes. To make matters worse, sometimes the actual dispute can easily be resolved. The ego won't let it be over until someone feels as if they've won.

In addition to the unspoken or disregarded baggage, the ego creates this power struggle in a dispute. Oddly enough, during conflict, it's often not about who's right or who's wrong, because generally speaking, people don't argue the facts. People argue and disagree because they feel they should be dominating the rights on the subject. They want to control the yeses and nos or how much and how often. They want to exude power. They want to have their way.

So why are we arguing? Well, because we haven't yet learned how to understand our behavioral triggers. On any given day, we're bringing emotional baggage to the table to sit with us while we're disputing. And as icing on the cake, we invite our egos to the negotiation table to throw tantrums and impede our progress toward amicable resolutions. Thus, my job becomes tougher to do. And the people who are trying to prove their points and get their way tighten their grips on their sides of the rope during tug-of-war.

"Sticks and Stones May Break My Bones, but Words Will Never Hurt Me" Is a Fallacy

As children, we're taught to diffuse situations where people say harsh words by using the rhyme "Sticks and stone my break my bones, but words will never hurt me." The idea of this rhyme is that words aren't as powerful as weapons; therefore, no matter which kinds of words are hurled in your direction, they shouldn't cause you harm. This, readers, is a big fat lie. Not only is it a lie, but it's also detrimentally misleading. It teaches people to listen to or absorb words with negative connotations and intentions, as long as you learn how to build yourself strong enough to deflect them. This is a serious instance of "psychological violence."

Psychological violence can be defined as anything that someone willingly does to another person to cause mental and emotional harm. During an intense dispute or negotiation, words are used very precisely, with every intention of conveying clear points of frustration, anger, disappointment, and of course, power. People want their words to hurt. They want people on the opposing side to feel the sting of their nonnegotiable points and their unwillingness to compromise, apologize, or be the bigger person. In instances where you can't put your hands on another person to show the complexity of your bruised feelings and ego, you want your words to hurt.

Brazen words with brutal effects stem from poor communication skills. When it comes to disputes, stronger and more effective communication skills can help remedy a conflict. The problem, however, is that people don't trust the communication process. They don't trust that the intentional listening, the mindful speaking, the tone, tongue, and timeliness of word choices will make a positive impact on how they resolve their disputes. Yes, effective communication is the most logical approach to reducing conflict, negotiating, and ending disputes, but truth be told, it's not always the quickest or most widely acceptable approach.

Today's fast-paced technological world drastically impacts effective communication. Not only can we say brazen words at lightning speed, but we can also say these things without being face-to-face, talking on the phone, or even being in the same time zone. Technology is increasing the speed of our communication but decreasing the quality of our communication. And when the quality of the way we communicate is impacted, the chances for disputes and conflict surge. The words, which we speak, do have the power to hurt people. And sometimes that's exactly what they're meant to do.

So Now What? How Can We Resolve Our Disputes and End Our Conflicts?

This book was designed to do two things: (1) point out the problems that exist in our communication within multiple areas of our lives, and (2) show you how to resolve them—almost like a professional. Upon reading this book, you will learn that whether your conflict is in a business setting, educational, romantic, religious, cultural, or personal, there's a very sound, smart, and simple method to resolving it. You'll discover that this system uses four foundational points, three pivotal moments, and six steps in order to reach an amicable resolve. And though it sounds like a hefty and long process, all these interconnected parts can take anywhere from two hours to six months to execute and see results. It all depends on how badly you would like to solve your problem.

As I've mentioned, I've been in this business a long time. However, I've also been married for a long time, a parent for a long time, and an employee for a long time. I've been exposed to my fair share of disputes and conflicts, some of which I care to forget and others that I believe made me a better communicator. Regardless, whether or not I made my point, "settled" the dispute, or maintained the relationship, I certainly learned a lot about myself, the people I associated with, and how to move on with my life after conflict.

Before I can begin to tell you how to resolve your conflicts or become a better problem solver, you'll need to know a bit more about yourself. As you recall, behavior is a key player in how disputes and conflicts arise. When you have a better idea about (1) who you are, (2) what your triggers are, and (3) how you respond to certain situations, then you'll be able to create a more effective strategy for participating in and ultimately resolving your problems.

So, prior to turning to the next page, I'd like to introduce you to the DISC test.[1]

Conflict resolution processes can be an effective tool if the parties are serious about resolving disputes. On the other hand, if emotional obstacles get in the way, whereby the parties are reluctant to resolve a matter, then it becomes impossible to resolve that dispute. Keep in mind that there are individuals who thrive on conflict and any attempt to resolve a dispute is a threat to their existence because being in conflict is part of their reason for existence.

On the other hand, if individuals truly want to resolve conflict, they must be willing to use the mirror on the wall and participate in self-examination. They must learn about themselves and how they deal with others, including personal issues, emotional stress, and anger, without destroying a good relationship with spouses, coworkers, and others.

[1] In the 1970s, John Geier, a faculty member in the University of Minnesota's Department of Health Sciences, used Self-Description to create the original Personal Profile System (PPS). He formed a company called Performax (which subsequently became Carlson Leaning Company, then Inscape Publishing, and is now part of Wiley) that was the first publisher of a DISC assessment.

So, prior to turning to the next page, I would like to introduce you to the DISC profile, a tool for self-examination. The DISC tool consists of four specific areas: (1) dominance, (2) influence, steadiness, and (4) conscientiousness. It offers individuals the opportunity to self-examine themselves on their various behavior styles at home, at work, and on the job.

Dominance

If you are a dominant coworker or team member, your strengths may include the ability to do the following:

- Can make a decision when no one else wants to
- Are not afraid to confront tough issues/situations
- Accept change as a personal challenge
- Keep the team focused and on task

Those who interact with you may see the following limitations:

- May come across as unapproachable
- Insensitive to others
- Impatient with others
- Try to get the team moving before it is ready

Influence

If you are an influential coworker or team member, your strengths may include the following:

- Are always available for others—give your time easily
- Are good at inspiring others
- Spread your enthusiasm and positive attitude to others
- Easily give positive feedback to those you work and interact with

Those you work with may see the following limitations:

- Disorganized
- Superficial in your approach
- Lack of follow-through
- Appear to not be focused on tasks

Steadiness

If you are a steady coworker or team member, your strengths may include that you are the following:

- A good team player
- Empathetic and sensitive to the needs of others
- Methodical and good at developing systems
- Good at learning
- Easy to get along with

Those who work with you may see the following limitations:

- Indecisive
- Indirect
- Resistant to change

Conscientiousness

If you are a conscientious coworker or team member, your strengths may include that you are the following:

- Thorough
- Certain to follow standards accurately
- Conscientious
- Diplomatic
- Accurate

Those who work with you may see the following limitations:

- Overly concerned with perfection

- Aloof

- Hampering creativity in others with your desire to stick to the rules

- Non-demonstrative

Conflict Resolution in Classrooms Could Curb Violence

The United States of America is the most advanced and powerful nation in the world when it comes to military preparedness, advanced technology, economics, and standard of living. With a few exceptions, we are holding our own and can compete globally in every area.

One area where we fall far short and lack any strategic plans for improvement is in our response to physical and psychological violence. We are fundamentally unable to grasp the essence and root causes of violence, and this prohibits us from seeking the appropriate solutions when dealing with violence and race relations.

Physical violence such as assault, rape, or murder is an extreme form of aggression. It's behavior in which physical force is exerted for the purpose of causing damage or injury. Psychological violence is anything that an individual or group does to knowingly harm others, be it verbally, mentally, morally, racially, criminally, sexually, or emotionally. Psychological violence is by and large rendered with the tongue; timing and tone can be as devastating as physical violence. The physically strongest person can be adversely injured by words.

In fact, gun violence is one of the most deadly components of violence. Approximately ninety individuals are gunned down through gun violence daily. Meanwhile, segregation and discrimination are rampant and appear to be acceptable as a way of life. We have the haves against the have-nots, whites against blacks, blacks against whites, rich against poor, males against females, religion against religion, young against old. All these conflicts are a form of violence.

Obviously, there is a reason for our failure in these areas. In my opinion, the basic reason for our failures and our reluctance to address these complex issues is, simply put, economics. Addressing this phenomenon is going to cost money, and most institutions are unwilling to make the investments.

In fact, our country is home to some of the most prestigious colleges and universities, each doing an excellent job preparing students for the world of work. However, we fail miserably when it comes to teaching our children how to manage conflict and deal with diversity. We fail to formally teach our children and advanced students how to manage and solve problems beyond the academic ones they encounter in the classroom. Managing conflict is a skill that can be taught to children and adults. Learning to solve conflict is like learning to swim or ride a bicycle. Once learned, you never forget it. Just think: children are not born violent. Violence is a learned behavior, and children by and large become a product of their environment. Children are not born hating others who don't look or worship like them. This hatred is taught to them as they grow up, and is passed along from generation to generation—similar to a rite of passage—by their elders for no rational reason other than meanness.

This behavior has now spilled over into all segments of our society, even politics, where it is now fashionable to stereotype individuals because of their religion, race, sex, sexual orientation, or nation's origin. This happens without any consequences, compassion, or feeling for those adversely affected by it.

In my opinion, one of the methods available to address the problem is within our reach. I believe that learning the humanistic approach to problem-solving at an early age is essential to our society's success and will ultimately save lives and money. Many of those who are incarcerated possibly could have avoided going to prison had they been taught some basic skills in resolving conflict. These skills could have been taught in our schools since most children are not taught problem-solving skills at home. Managing conflict and diversity should be a mandatory part of the school curriculum because it will better prepare our children for the real world. Children need to be taught the importance of self-examination, forgiveness, apology, compassion, and developing good listening skills in order to become a holistic person.

Because of the size of the problem and the limitation on teachers and administrators in terms of discipline, there has to be a different approach. I believe that in order to address this critical problem, every school district should implement a mandatory conflict-resolution training program for grades K-12. I recognize that there are costs involved. I also realize this recommendation is not the ultimate panacea. However, if implemented in our schools, a conflict-resolution training program would pay tremendous dividends, ultimately saving lives and money and, in some instances, preventing incarceration.

We can do better.

Note from Hez

Education

Bullying and Gang and Gun Violence
"So What?"

Another reason that influenced me to write this book was the continuous inability of our society to address the issues of physical and psychological violence among our youth and adults. It is apparent to me that the government, politicians, criminal justice system, hiring more policemen, building more jails is not an effective process.

Therefore, I decided to offer a few solutions and recommendations on how to address this global issue. It has a devastating impact on our schools and communities on a daily basis. I was further motivated to write this book after reading the local newspapers and watching the local television report the news regarding gun violence, gangs, and bullying. In fact, there is hardly a single day that passes in which we do not hear of young children and adults being killed or wounded by gunfire. Just this past week, it was reported that a four-year-old child was attending church service and was hit by a stray bullet. It is time for us as a community to start to take some action in assisting in eradicating the problem. *If not now, when? If not us, who?*

The United States of America is still the most powerful and sophisticated nation in *the world*. We have been successful in making advanced technology, putting a man on the moon, planting satellites in space, and leading the world in social development. Unfortunately, this has not trickled down to the young people in our local communities.

Somehow, these advances seem to escape the various communities, especially in our schools and minority communities. Violence, bullying, and conflict seem to be a way of life in our schools. Our children seem to lack the social skills needed to handle and manage these issues. Let's take a look at bullying, for example—a pervasive issue in our schools. Recent statistics around bullying are frightening:

- 8% of students miss one day of school per month.
- 43% fear harassment in school bathrooms.
- 80% of the time, arguments with a bully result in physical altercations.
- 30% of students heard another student threaten to kill someone.
- 20% of students know of other students who bring guns to school.
- Every seven minutes, a child is bullied, increasing violence on school grounds.
- Each month, 282,000 students are physically attacked in schools.
- Most of the violence actually occurs on school grounds.

Analyzing this data produces frightening revelations. Our children are losing the battle. They are on the front line of the American social conflict.

I believe that by teaching young people the values associated with managing conflict, we address other issues that may be lacking. We should teach children the values of compassion, forgiveness, and the humility associated with the art of apologizing for behavior that negatively affects others.

Most of us send our children (or minors that we care for) to school. We help them with their homework, attend the parent-teacher conferences, go to their ceremonies, and do all the things we're supposed to do when it comes to preparing them to become great students. As parents or guardians, we understand the importance of education. We try to shape their minds and motivate them to understand the importance of their education as well.

There's nothing wrong with being the parent that sends their child to school to learn and become the best thinker that they can become. However, school is not just a place of learning and churning out assignments. School is also a place for social engagement and developing relationship-building skills. It's one of the places where a child's character begins to form and where they experience the most social pressure and mental development. School is beyond the books and the projects. School is where your child learns how to deal with a variety of people of different ages, backgrounds, and personality types who live in their community.

Our children are interacting with adults and their peers for at least seven hours a day for five days a week. You would think we'd pay extra attention to the quality of those encounters and teach them how to deal with conflict. However, this is not the case. Most children don't learn how to deal with conflict until they're facing it or after it's already happened. So while they're at school learning reading, writing, and arithmetic, they're also probably encountering conflict. This would be in the form of bullying, losing friends, not fitting in, or not properly respecting their authoritative figures. Yet if they come home with good grades and merit awards, as parents or guardians, we may not notice the problem until it's too late.

It would be nice to think that childhood conflict doesn't appear in school-aged children until secondary school or later. However, this is a fallacy. From the moment we drop our children off at school for the very first time, we are placing them in situations where they will not only face academic challenges but they'll also face social challenges. While some challenges may be greater than others and not all challenges will warrant extreme disciplinary action, the fact is, these challenges may turn into conflicts. And our children rarely know how to deal with those conflicts.

To take it a step further, early on in life, children learn the chant "Sticks and stones may break my bones, but words will never hurt me." This couldn't be farther from the truth. This chant has good intentions, but honestly, it doesn't actually speak to or even remotely resolve the hurt feelings, anger, and frustration that our children feel when their peers taunt them with maleficent words. In fact, hurtful speech is one of the biggest acts of psychological violence that our children endure during their early childhood education. The amount of teasing and taunting that goes on during a school day is more than enough for their fragile minds and emotions to deal with. Yet we don't actually teach them how to deal with these threats to their social development and personal happiness. Instead most of us resort to the same old chant of "Sticks and stones may break my bones, but words will never hurt me."

We should be teaching them that words do hurt sometimes. While we can't let these words stop us from pursuing greater things, we do need to learn how to deal with hateful or emotionally draining speech. Furthermore, we need to teach them how to deal with the social, emotional, and physical conflicts that could arise from this type of speech. Teaching children to ignore the words only suppresses the need to respond. It doesn't help them identify, reply, and remedy the situation in a mature and amicable manner. And although you may be thinking "My five-year-old son/daughter wouldn't understand what that process means!" the truth is, they probably would.

We don't give our children enough credit for their ability to receive high-level information and process it according to their own maturity levels. Also, we don't take enough time to give them the information, even if it takes multiple attempts for them to understand it. They need help to process information according to their own maturity levels. So what tends to happen is, we delay the conversations, education, and training about conflict and dispute resolution. Unfortunately, we end up sitting in the principal's office, or worse, the police station, questioning how things got so bad and what could've been done to prevent this.

At the onset of their educational journeys, we should be teaching our children how to deal with people who think, behave, or speak indifferently toward them. We shouldn't be telling them to ignore it or get over it. Instead we should be honest about how it makes them feel and how they should approach and respond to it. And yes, this can be taught to a child in preschool. In fact, have you ever observed young children (between the ages of three and five years old) engage with their peers? It can be one of the most joyful yet complex observances. The range in their emotions and interactions will show you that young children definitely need to learn how to resolve their own conflicts—especially before overprotective parents get involved. From snatching toys and not sharing to taunting, throwing tantrums, and being defiant, these traits are a part of self-expression and social development. Yet they're also an indicator that there's a conflict that the child hasn't been taught to handle.

Our children are automatically subjected to dealing with people and learning how to manage their relationships, yet they aren't taught what to do when a conflict occurs. We teach them how to physically defend themselves at a young age (even going as far as showing them the proper way to hold their fists and land a punch). However, we don't do the prerequisite work of teaching them how to resolve their problems before they turn into physical altercations. To make matters worse, we'll defend our children in the principal's office or anywhere else when they've responded in a physical altercation, with statements such as "The other kid started it!" or "I told my child not to let anyone put their hands on them!" or "He/she was defending themselves during the attack!" However, how often do we hold ourselves accountable, as parents or guardians, and admit that had we taught them to resolve conflicts with maturity and level-headedness, perhaps none of this would've happened in the first place?

How do we teach our children the importance of conflict resolution when they're inundated with school work and extracurricular activities and we're inundated with adult responsibilities? There are two steps to making this happen. First, it's important that school systems integrate conflict resolution into their lesson planning. Taking fifteen minutes out of each day to teach children (1) how to think and respond with maturity, (2) how to approach conflict, (3) steps to resolve their conflicts, and (4) how to move on after conflict—this could actually prevent consequences such as in-school or out-of-school suspension, infraction citing, and even expulsion.

Think about it, fifteen minutes of "what to do to handle conflicts" dialogue and training results in seventy-five minutes of training per week. This adds up to about five hours of training per month and forty hours of training within a school year. It doesn't take away from the rest of their critical learning needs, but it can reduce the amount of time that teachers, administrators, and parents can spend with dealing with the grievances of a child who has been engaged in a conflict. It can reduce the amount of time teachers spend on breaking up fights and arguments. It can reduce the overhead expenses for security measures such as surveillance cameras, metal detectors, and security guards in the school. Fifteen minutes of conflict resolution education can prevent the physical, emotional, and social damages. This is usually caused by children not knowing how to deal with their conflicts because they haven't been taught.

In addition, those same fifteen minutes can be used at home. As parents, we can have conversations about how to respond to negative speech and actions—far beyond ignoring it or throwing up their fists. The unique thing about teaching our children about conflict resolution at home is that we can show our children, through their own behaviors and dialogue, what they should and should not be doing. The next time there's a sibling brawl, instead of taking sides, yelling, breaking up the fight, or punishing your children, ask them what happened and how they could've handled it differently. Walk them through the mediation process by establishing neutral ground (the kitchen table or your family room is a great place for this). Ask them to individually address their grievances, giving them both ample time to speak their minds and state the problem; but don't allow them to talk across the table or engage in a verbal brawl. Then ask them to explain how it made them feel or why they responded the way that they did. Ask them about what would make things better between them and how to execute those details. Finally, ask them to agree to the resolution or propose a different one. Once they agree on the resolution, not only has the problem been dealt with in a mature manner, but you've also taught them how to deal with future conflicts using tried-and-true conflict resolution approaches.

It's time to introduce conflict resolution into our children's regular education—in school and at home. We're living in an age where information spreads so quickly and our children are constantly stimulated and triggered by the programming from their electronic devices, entertainment, and peer pressure. Without proper conflict resolution training, especially within our children's regular learning routines, we're not preparing our children to be mature, responsible, well-meaning, and respectable children and then adults. We can no longer afford to tell them that words won't hurt them or to put up their fists, because words are increasingly becoming more hateful and traveling faster and farther with things like social media and text messages. And fists are the last things that kids are thinking about in a physical altercation—now they respond with weapons. A simple and intentional conversation and training on identifying, preventing, and ultimately resolving conflict resolution not only makes our children well-equipped people, it could also help save their lives.

Note from Hez

Race

In my lifetime, I have lived and worked through a difficult era. I survived prejudice, discrimination, oppression, and stereotyping in my work years. Most of my professional career as a mediator and arbitrator involved working with a diverse community.

I can recall being told that African American mediators were not acceptable in certain parts of the United States because of the color of their skin. African American mediators were primarily assigned to large urban cities in New York, California, and Midwestern states. In later years, African Americans were assigned to large cities like Atlanta, Georgia.

In addition, I can recall being discriminated against while seeking housing for my family in New York City. I can recall the N-word being used in my presence while mediating disputes. I can recall one of my white colleagues calling me several derogatory names. He used every racial epithet known to mankind in order to degrade me in the presence of a predominately white audience. The only punishment the individual received was a "good ole boy" response stating that he had a little too much to drink. However, I learned in my earlier life that when an individual says something when they are under the influence of alcohol, it is just their true feelings being revealed.

Moreover, all of those incidents were very challenging. However, I refused to respond to any of the incidents of racism because I knew how to turn a negative into a positive. Had I responded in a violent manner, in all probability, my career would not have culminated to the degree that it did. It projected me into becoming the first African American appointed to serve as chairman of the New York State Mediation Board.

I was appointed by Governor Mario Cuomo and confirmed by the New York Senate. I had offices in Buffalo, Syracuse, Albany, Long Island, and New York City. The two other board members and all the professional staff were white. This was another challenge for me where I encountered racial problems. Some of the staff were absolutely reluctant to respond to directives from me and stated that they would not cooperate with me and they would watch me slowly twist away.

However, they were unsuccessful in seeing me slowly twist away, and I successfully managed the merger of the New York State Labor Relations Board and the New York State Mediation Board, which saved the State of New York a tremendous amount of funds. I added free arbitration and mediation training to individuals who worked in the labor relations field. I developed training for the support staff and essentially increased the professionalism of the agencies. Some of those individuals who were reluctant to take orders from an African American retired or transferred to other agencies.

Many individuals have asked me how I successfully survived working in a predominately white world during my career. My response is very simple: "I valued my job, and I had a family depending on my income." I realized early in life that every statement made in your presence does not require a response. I was adamant about not permitting others to define who I am. I learned at an early age that if you respond to name-calling, you are permitting others to define who you are. If you know who you are, no one can define who you are by calling you a name.

In addition, I learned that hard work pays off and race becomes less of a factor. When African Americans are given the opportunity to demonstrate and utilize their skills the same as other races, African Americans can become a huge success.

It must be noted that racism is alive and continues to raise its ugly head, even in churches and synagogues across the country. In fact, there are 1,900 known racist/hate groups in the United States, and the number is growing.

Many individuals believe that we are no longer engaged in discrimination, prejudice, oppression, and suppression because an African American was twice elected to presidency. That kind of thinking is antiquated and vastly exaggerated because President Barack Obama has faced more adversity and obstruction than any other president in the history of our country. In fact, he and the First Lady were caricatured as chimpanzees on social media. In the history of our country, no other president has had as many appointments filibustered as President Obama. Of all the forty-three presidents, only eighty-six appointments were filibustered. Under Obama, eighty-two appointments were filibustered in five years.

Furthermore, we cannot forget the fact that on the day of President Obama's first inauguration, a large number of highly elected officials had a meeting and made a pledge that they would not cooperate with the president, claiming "nothing would be accomplished under his presidency." They went on to say he would be a one-term president. Others stated they hope he fails. Some suggest that part of the problem is trust. Per one study, only one-third of the public now say they have trust in their fellow Americans. About half felt that way in 1972 when the general survey was done. Some blame this on the polarized politicians: Democrats against Republicans, Conservatives against Liberals, the Independents and the Tea Party against all of the above.

One of the things I have noticed over the past sixty-two years is that the United States Congress and the Supreme Court have tried to legislate and litigate fairness through civil and equal rights. Congress has passed antidiscrimination laws addressing voting rights, housing, employment, civil rights, affirmative action, and equal employment opportunity. (It must be noted that African Americans are the only race of people to arrive in the United States and laws have to be passed for rights that others enjoy because of the color of their skin.) The intention behind this legislation is positive. However, evidence shows that it is extremely difficult to litigate or pass legislation on how individuals deal with someone they have been taught to dislike, as demonstrated by the treatment of President Obama.

Children are not born prejudiced or disliking others who are different. They are taught through tradition, culture, and so-called family values to dislike others who are different. In fact, this prejudicial thinking is passed on like a rite of passage from generation to generation. One of the most significant issues missed by the good-faith legislation is the humanistic part. Passing legislation without a component that brings people together has proven that legislators will do what they must do until the next election where the positive and good-intention legislation is challenged and watered down and down and ultimately becomes insignificant and ineffective.

In this chapter, we'll discuss how to navigate racially driven conflicts while maintaining a sense of pride and appreciation of our racial culture of differences.

Resolving Racial Disputes

America is a melting pot of cultures and races. The country is made up of people from all around the world. They have come to this great country because of its reputation for freedom and opportunity. With all these different cultural backgrounds come different beliefs, practices, and preconceived notions. Although we share the same land, honor the same flag, and live under the same Constitution, our differences in skin color and ethnicities seems to be the things that keep us apart and serve as a foundation for our biggest conflicts.

Sometimes it seems like no matter what the argument is, if it occurs between two different races, the underlying conflict has a lot to do with skin color. It doesn't matter if two people are in a disagreement about wages, rules, operational procedures, or workplace grievances. If that argument is between an African American person and a white person, or an Asian and a Latino, the underlying issue of race relations rears its ugly head.

I was the tenth black person to serve as a federal mediator in the history of the agency. During my tenure as a mediator, I've seen and heard how preconceived dispositions and learned behaviors can cause huge grievances between people. The characteristics that someone feels that they know about another race and how that race responds, thinks, and feels, leads to some of the more ignorant conversations. Whether I've come to the table fully prepared to mediate terms or listen to everyone's side of the story, it will not make a difference if their prejudices show up at the table too. Race is one of those topics that need to be handled delicately. The conversation can very easily transition from a casual talk to a heated debate or physical altercation if the wrong words are uttered.

How Does Race Start an Argument?

Why is race such a sensitive topic? Why does it lead to such animosity or serve as the foundation for such major differences? It's because, primarily, we as a people haven't been taught to accept everyone's differences. Additionally, we use race as the measure of our value and others' values. Somewhere along the way in our lives, we are made to believe that skin color not only makes one person different than the other, but it also makes one better than the other.

Believe it or not, usually within the first ten seconds of meeting someone, we've formed an opinion of who they are and what they are all about. Of course, these opinions are extremely superficial because we don't have enough information on the person to really know them. However, we use this information as the foundation of building and discarding a relationship with them, our intentions, and ultimately their value in our lives. These opinions are deeply rooted in assumptions of their character and abilities. Furthermore, they are secured by our preconceived notions about their race.

Racial discrimination has a strong foundation in assumption. People assume that one person has a pile of positive or negative characteristics because of the depth of their melanin or pigmentation. Oftentimes, it has nothing to do with their education, their upbringing, their religion, or even their favorite color. Racial discrimination is built on an impenetrable amount of assumption. As I mentioned in the beginning of this book, when people feel that they "know what they know" and that they're right (ego), it can lead to some of the lengthiest disputes and most complicated arguments to resolve.

Why Do We Feel the Way We Do about Race?

From an early age, people are taught that one race is worse than another. When children start questioning the differences between hair texture, facial features, skin color, and language, they are given explanations that are rooted in race. On top of that, some children are taught, at that very moment, that people with these features are less valuable or have negative characteristics because of these differences. From that point on, children start changing the way they look at people who are different from them. It no longer has anything to do with their physical attributes alone.

Unfortunately, children carry these prejudices and assumptions until they reach an age of maturity and beyond. These notions can be dispelled when they are taught something different. If no one ever challenges their upbringing or introduces them to diversity, they become adults with prejudices who are stuck in their ways of thinking despite the jobs that they have, the political position that they hold, or the countless number of times that they've been proven wrong about their prejudices.

Racism is alive and well because it never stopped being taught through generation after generation, similar to a rites-of-passage doctrine. Although it may not be formally taught (through education and training), it's socially taught through conversation, media, music, and the relationships we cultivate with others. Every day, we encounter some piece of information that encourages us to continue conversations that divide us according to our skin color. Depending on what we were taught as children or urged to believe during our upbringing, we either embrace this information or discard it.

To add another layer of depth to our feelings about race, we are also systematically segregated. This is where the real problem lies. There are social, political, and economic systems that have maintained their strength based on a system of segregation. These systems are formed and meant to keep us divided. They are so complex and have various technical nuances that regular everyday folks like us can't even begin to fathom. These systems are generational and deeply embedded in the fibers of our country. They continue to thrive and shape the way that our laws, school systems, political systems, financial systems, neighborhoods, and communities function.

Race is both on the surface area and hidden within our conflicts. When we're arguing (specifically about race), it is blatantly in our faces, holding us to our versions of the truth and reminding us about the ways of "those other people." When we're arguing about topics completely unrelated to race, we're paying attention to every detail of the opposing person, subconsciously believing that what they feel has everything to do with their skin color. Race causes us to have these irrefutable opinions, such as what another person's standards and values are; we then use those opinions to judge them. Therefore, during our conflicts with others, we spend so much of our time rebutting those opinions while trying to get to the root of our problems.

How Do We Solve Racial Tensions during Conflicts?

Changing the color of our skin and genetic makeup isn't an option for resolving our racial tensions. We must learn how to solve our conflicts in a more reasonable manner. The fact is, the melting pot of the society that we live in isn't going to change any time soon. So if we don't learn how to solve our problems with people who look different from us, we'll be having problems for the rest of our lives.

When we find ourselves having these conflicts, there are two things we must remember. First, we must participate and find common ground within our discussion; second, we must argue based on what is actually going on. Using these two steps will help us avoid using race as a scapegoat for our disagreements. It will keep us focused on resolving the issue at hand.

Participating in the argument and finding common ground forces us to be mature and open-minded. There are so many instances within a discussion where the lack of these characteristics causes a snowball effect in the conflict. Words, behaviors, and responses begin to build up and escalate the conflict to something else. Finding common ground reminds us of our humanity in time of indecency. It's okay to banter, but at our core, we must respect each other based on the things we have in common—no matter how small or insignificant they may be.

In addition to this step, we must also argue the facts. I can't recall the number of instances in my career that I've had to remind people that we're resolving an actual issue that has a *real* background and *real* consequences. There is no point in arguing about things that do not matter because resolving those things ultimately will not matter. It's more critical that we remember to argue based on what is *actually* going on, so that we may solve the problem at hand.

However, to participate in the argument, find common ground and argue about the facts. A prerequisite *must* be filled. We must come to the table with a knowledge of ourselves. It's important to know who we are as individuals before we can either argue with intelligence and competence or resolve things amicably and with dignity. Self-knowledge is critical during conflict resolution. People tend to use negative information, judgments, and assumptions within the tone and timing of their words to cause harm. If you are not secure in who you are, with the ability to discern between psychological violence and truth, you can easily be affected by what others say about you. In addition, we must be able to implement and define the following issues in addressing racial problems.

Six Things We Must Learn to Live With

Here are four things: having self-knowledge, participating, finding common ground, and arguing the facts. These core behaviors will lead to resolving any conflict, mainly the one dealing with race. However, I've come to learn that there are six other things that one should learn to deal with before they engage in disputes regarding race or discrimination. If evaluated and executed properly, the following six factors will keep opposing parties on neutral ground, despite their differences.

1. **Learn to deal with the self.** We must be honest with ourselves about who we are, how we think, and what we believe. We must also know why we are the way we are, as well as why we think and believe what we do. Self-examination helps us measure how far we've come and how far we must go to become people we are proud of and become the best version of ourselves.

2. **Learn to deal with others.** We're individuals who share the same geographical and social spaces with others. Therefore, we must learn how to deal with other people. We must understand the importance of our relationships with other people so that we can exchange positions with one another to increase our compassion. Although we have our differences, which range from religious beliefs to physical appearances, we must learn how to treat others and always be respectful.

3. **Learn to live with challenges.** By learning every single day, there will be situations that force us to make tough decisions. We interact with people who look and think differently from the way we do. We may respond to situations we don't necessarily feel like participating in, but we're training ourselves to deal with challenges. We can try to prepare for our challenges, but some things occur long before we're prepared to deal with them. That's what makes them challenges. And these challenges are things that strengthen and define our character.

4. **Learn to acknowledge change.** Change is one of the most difficult things for people to adjust to. We're creatures of habit, and we typically adapt these habits during our primary years. We are exposed to vast amounts of information. We form our opinions and personalities in a way that we almost become immune to change. We must become change agents because change is inevitable and awaits no one. When it comes to race relations, change helps us dispel our preconceived notions and improve how we relate to others.

5. **Learn to live your choice.** Choices are tricky, and until we become knowledgeable about ourselves and others, we'll make choices that are not deeply rooted in facts and sound judgment. Our choices can impact us for the rest of our life. Therefore, we must educate ourselves on facts that we can stand by, instead of assumptions and opinions that can easily be proven wrong or biased. Living with our choices requires us to be mature because we must also be willing to live with the consequences of our choices.

6. **Learn to live with conflict.** Finally, like challenges, we can try our best to prepare for things, but conflict happens when we least expect it. We may not be able to avoid our conflicts, but we can certainly resolve them with decency and competency. Things won't always be peaceful, nor will every resolution come peacefully. However, when we accept that conflict will happen, we can also accept that we'll do our part to manage the conflict with as much respect as possible.

Solving racial conflicts will remain difficult unless we learn how to deal with ourselves and others. Not only do we have to learn how to deal with these things, we must also respect our differences. Do not use them as a reason to treat people as less valuable or powerful than another person. In addition, we can no longer allow race to be an undertone or a disagreement with others. It cannot be the culprit that makes our arguments unresolvable or our positions more substantiated than others. Race cannot be the elephant in the room. It cannot be the reason why we cannot come to the table with facts and substantial reasoning. Otherwise, we still cannot see eye to eye.

Building Bridges for a Better Understanding through Education and Communication

GLOBAL AND HOLISTIC METHODS TO ADDRESS THE CURRENT PROBLEMS FACING OUR COMMUNITIES

There are four basic problems that need to be addressed in order to solve the problems between law enforcement and the minority communities. They are as follows:

1. Systemic and institutional *bias*. Systemic and institutional bias must be carefully addressed in a manner that will point out the detriments of this epidemic and offer specific solutions to the problem. It must be acknowledged that the vast majority of law enforcement officers in the United States perform their job with pride and honor. It is a small percentage that engages in unlawful acts that have a negative impact on all law enforcement personnel. It must

be further acknowledged that law enforcement departments are not different from other institutions and corporations throughout the United States. It is a small percentage of individuals in almost every institution/cooperation and community who violate the rules and regulations, which permeate throughout the institutions, and everyone gets judged by the activity of a few.

2. Education and training. Law enforcement officers must be educated on the four Rs—rights, restrictions, responsibility, and respect. Law enforcement officers must understand that every citizen has specific rights under the United States Constitution, state laws, and local laws. In order to get respect, one must be capable of practicing the same. Law enforcement officers must recognize that they are restricted by law from violating citizens' rights. Law enforcement officers must understand that they have a basic responsibility to uphold the law and not abuse it. Law enforcement officers must be taught and utilized as pointed out in other parts of this book. The officers and all stakeholders must be involved in designing the program at all levels. Must be buy-in in all levels. Law enforcement officers should be involved in designing training programs. Need and assessment must be performed prior to implementing programs.

3. Grand jury. Many believe that the current American grand jury system has largely become a prosecutor's rubber stamp. Prosecutors are unwilling to take on the police department because they work with the police week in and week out. The law gives the policemen a lot of discretion. If a police officer reasonably believes a suspect is putting someone in serious danger, they can use deadly force. Given those circumstances, the recent actions of the grand jury system have demonstrated that it lacks credibility to do what it was designed to do. Therefore, the entire system must be examined to assure individuals and communities that the system is not tainted because grand juries do not see all of the evidence. They

only see what the prosecutor wants them to see. There is no defense or opposing attorneys present to challenge any evidence through cross-examination, nor is there an independent judge to verify that there is fairness and equity in the evident submitted.

4. While many are advocating training for law enforcement officers, there are other parts of the equation that will be missing. Training law enforcement officers and failing to even acknowledge that others need training in a wide variety of topics would be equivalent to placing a football player that never played football on the football field and expecting him to perform at an acceptable level. Therefore, we believe that because of racial tension that has been created by the Ferguson, Missouri, Staten Island, New York, and Baltimore incidents, we believe that training should be advocated across the board. The corporate world, the communities, and the schools should implement like training. In fact, in order to address the problems, school districts should implement managing conflict K-12 in schools to prepare the youth of tomorrow for the future. In that training, students should be taught the role of the law enforcement officer and how to react when faced with a crisis situation, including their rights as law-abiding citizens. The four Rs would be appropriate— rights, restriction, responsibility, and respect.

Note from Hez

Managing Our Relationship

I have been married to the same wonderful, understanding, forgiving, loving, supportive, outstanding mother, grandmother, and compassionate woman for fifty-seven years. Her name is Zelma Christine Brown. We married on April 23, 1960, while we were very young. The only thing we knew was that we were in love and wanted to spend the rest of our lives together. We danced to an old love song, "Love Is a Many-Splendored Thing," recorded by Andy Williams and the Four Aces. The words in this song are so profound and beautiful, they capture the true feeling when you meet someone and fall in love.

This song explains how many young and elderly couples feel when they first meet and fall in love. They really believe that "love is a many-splendored thing," and they truly believe that they really love each other, until they have their first child and first financial crisis. Apparently, something happens to that love that is a many-splendored thing! In fact, the blame game starts, which creates unsolvable, simple misunderstandings. In most instances, the parties are unable to deal with unforeseen problems because they are inexperienced in dealing with problems and end up pointing fingers at each other and end up in divorce court. They fail to take advantage of anger and the far-reaching negative implications of refusing or failing to understand the humanistic part of conflict. It's okay to get angry and have conflict, because "making up" is wonderful, relaxing, and emotional.

In fact, many individuals predicted we would not remain married for an extended period because we were and still are two different people. I was outgoing and enjoyed people, played sports too long, worked long hours, and continue to be active in my community. She is just the opposite—she didn't understand sports and never joined any professional organizations or sororities. She remained the same. However, she became active in church and was ordained a deaconess in the African Methodist Episcopal Zion Church and modified her position and will tolerate some special people. She enjoys eating out but still enjoys being home.

In this process, we learned some valuable lessons that contributed to our successful marriage. We learned early about the art of compromise, forgiveness, allowing for mistakes, and acknowledging that no one is perfect. In addition, we learned that God gave us two ears and one mouth, which means that individuals are supposed to listen more than they talk, and the one that talks the loudest is very seldom heard.

Moreover, in many instances, individuals selfishly opt to separate or divorce, which has a devastating impact on children and family. In fact, some individuals start a new relationship and even remarry, carrying that same anger over into the new relationship (including keeping the conflict going with the ex).

In this chapter, we'll discuss how to manage our relationship to maintain positive communication, even during time of difficulty and conflict.

Relationships

There are various reasons to argue or find something wrong with your spouse, which leads to conflict. So when you and your spouse are emotionally involved in a heated argument, just when you think you have to respond, just when you think you have the answer, just when you think you have the opposing party trapped, *shut up*. The reason and rationale is simple. Generally speaking, you are never going to resolve a dispute when both parties are angry and not listening to each other. It's like quicksand—the more you say, the deeper in you get.

Isn't it strange how individuals fall in and out of love? Not because they don't love each other, but because they lose the ability to communicate in a respectful and peaceful manner. It is a result of being ill-equipped to resolve conflict. It's easy to point the finger at the other person without accepting any responsibility for the conflict. It is also easy to walk away from a relationship and have both parties suffer, including children and other family members.

This is primarily the reason for the high number of separations and divorce. In fact, 50% of those getting married in 2016–2017 will end up in divorce. This isn't a new statistic, but it certainly is a shocking one. If couples who met, spent months dating or courting each other, spent thousands of dollars on their special wedding day, and accumulated martial debts and assets knew that they were

50 percent likely to end up in divorce, how many of them would subject themselves to that kind of luck? The truth is, many of them still would. Getting married could also lead to getting divorced. When a couple communicates well and learns how to deal with the roller coasters of marriage, chances are, they won't wind up in divorce court.

Relationships experience problems. There is no clear understanding of how to resolve their problems, or they don't understand the significance of understanding their problems. Traits such as selfishness, reluctance to deal with their issues, envy, and jealousy are the main culprits that split relationships apart. In addition to these negative attributes is relying on the ill-fated family tradition of how to handle things. Here is an example: "My mother or father behaved like this, so I'm going to do it too!" That is a very quick way to break up a relationship. When a couple (especially a married one) is unwilling to make sacrifices and reverse their negative attributes for the sake of a relationship, it's doomed to fail. In their mind, it's easier to divorce than to resolve.

Personality aside, a core issue in maintaining a healthy relationship or marriage is managing finances. Money has a way of creating division in a relationship. Arguments about budgeting, spending, saving, and earning will always surface, even when a couple is wealthy. Money can become a power struggle, especially if one person contributes the most or more frequently than the other. And when it comes down to what to do with the money, the problems just seem to escalate. However, just because money becomes a pain point in a relationship doesn't mean it must be a constantly dragging force that leads to the demise of the marriage or a friendship. Like dealing with negative traits, a couple needs to establish neutral ground or a problem-solving mechanism to solve their problems— even before they begin.

It is impossible to resolve a dispute when two people are angry. It sounds weird when you evaluate this statement. However, anger has a way of creating wedges in communication and altering the way people behave. When a person is angry, they are the least rational, which means that they are least likely to employ problem-solving mechanisms to resolve their disputes. That's why it's critical that a couple undergo counseling in the beginning or create a plan to identify when there's a problem and methods to get to the root of it then resolve it.

A good solution as the first mechanism to resolving a dispute is to stop talking. When people are engaged in combative dialogue, their problems intensify. So instead of dealing with one main issue, a couple is now threatened with attitudes, subproblems, hurt feelings, and more.

Additionally, the combative dialogue can incite psychologically violent ways, simply because two people with bruised egos and differing opinions haven't begun to work out their problems. The decision to cease talking means that both parties are giving themselves room to focus on their issues versus focus on retaliation.

The prerequisite for handling any problem in a mature and dignified manner is checking your ego at the door. It doesn't matter who's right or wrong, who starts the argument, who's the most impacted by the dispute, or anything else for that matter. When you're trying to outlay your problems and resolve them, the ego should not be allowed to enter the conversation, or the room for that matter.

In my experience as a mediator, I have learned to rely on three steps to help people walk away from a conflict. The most important factor of these three steps is that they all require strong communication skills. It takes time to develop good communication skills, especially in a marriage, but it can be done. That's why it's critical that certain mechanisms be installed at the onset of a relationship. Communication skills naturally evolve and become stronger over time, versus being the make-or-break of an argument or a marriage.

One step that couples can use to walk away from a conflict is self-examination. Both individuals in a relationship should take time to be honest with themselves about who they are. How did they contribute to the problem? When they know what the foundation of the situation is, they are increasing their chances of dissolving their egos and resolving their problems. Self-examination should be an immediate follow-up to temporarily ceasing conversation.

Next, people should be able to exchange positions with the other side. Most times, especially in a heated argument, people only see things from their point of view (another way that the ego creeps up and into a dispute). This one-sided perspective usually always paints one person as a victim and the other person as a villain. However, if people learn how to exchange perspectives and put themselves in the other person's shoes, they can begin to see an alternative perspective. This exchange can shed new light on a dispute and bring it closer to resolution.

Finally, and most importantly, people should rely on good listening skills. Listening is an art that requires more than opening your ears and nodding your head in agreement when appropriate. Listening is about using sympathy and empathy, exchanging perspectives, and honing in on what the other person is trying to communicate. It means not talking or preparing to respond or retaliate while the other person is talking. Again, it's one of those skills that really take time to develop.

These three steps, when used intentionally and with the hope of resolving a problem, can help people in a relationship solve a dispute. In addition to employing these steps, a couple needs to be upfront about very specific issues that relate to their marriage. The most common arguments seem to arise because these issues were never fully discussed, agreed on, and planned for before they became issues.

People in a committed relationship need to discuss having children. Whether they're in the intermediate stages of their dating relationship, on their way to the altar, or a few months into the marriage, deciding on children is an incredible conversation that shouldn't be avoided. Things like how many children to have, whether they want certain responsibilities related to child rearing, and how to raise them. These issues need to be fully discussed before the pregnancy announcements and certainly before childbirth.

Infidelity is a topic that makes people uncomfortable. It's a topic that people don't like to confess to or even like to deal with. The idea of cheating or being unfaithful seems like an irreversible act. However, that's not always the case—especially when a couple discusses how to handle it. Marriage often means allowing for mistakes and never saying "never." People in a relationship cheat for many various reasons. And although it's not right, it can be forgivable. This is something that must be discussed, in terms of how to handle the discussion and the healing process, before someone admits to cheating or infidelity is discovered.

In all, problem-solving, especially in a relationship, is a planned procedure. There are many methods that could work, but they all depend on the couple, their personalities, their conversation style, and what they want to accomplish. The point is, maintaining a healthy relationship that can endure hardship and disputes requires people who can engage in effective dialogue. They need to be able to inquire, learn, offer their thoughts, and discover a shared vision.

Here are six additional steps that a couple can use to resolve their problems:

1. Design a mutual place/time to have complicated discussions.

2. Say something nice about the other person and recall the positive things about the relationship.

3. Talk about their behavior and what you'd like to see change. Also, discuss the consequences of not deciding to change.

4. Let the other person speak and listen to them. Don't show emotion, even if you disagree with what is being said.

5. Thank them for the meeting.

6. Agree to reconvene in a specified time to monitor changes and review what has been said.

Solving Religious Disputes

There are probably three topics that are extremely difficult to discuss with people, and those three topics are money, politics, and religion. Perhaps these topics are extremely sensitive because people hold their ideologies close to their hearts. Or perhaps these topics are extremely sensitive because people don't know how to accept each other's differences. This is especially true when it comes to the subject of religion and learning how to resolve disputes about our religious differences.

If you put ten people in a room and ask them about their religious beliefs, you may find that many of them share a common ground. They may believe in one creator. They may agree on the day of the week that church service should be held. They might even agree on many of the rules and parables of a religious book. However, if you were to begin to probe into their personal feelings, experiences, ideas, theories, or practices regarding religion, this is when disputes and disagreements are likely to arise. It's perfectly acceptable for people to have different ideas and methods to practice their religious beliefs. The problem is *how* people discuss their differences, deal with them, and agree to disagree.

The topic of religion is so sensitive that it even has deep-rooted issues within the building where it's supposed to be safe to discuss it—the church. Have you ever been to a church meeting and witnessed a religious disagreement between leaders or members? Considering the environment and the topic, you'd think that their discrepancies could be amicably resolved. Oftentimes, it's not. Discussing religion has a way of putting people on edge and making them defensive. Naturally, if they're defensive, their words may become harsher as they try to protect their beliefs and feelings about the topic. This creates the perfect storm for a dispute to erupt and for people to lose sight of their goals to encourage others to use their own religious beliefs to deal with the situations in their lives.

People hold their religious and spiritual beliefs with high regard, and rightfully so. However, as a society, we are very quick to be condemning and judgmental of people with opinions who differ from our own. And religion has no exception. Whether our differences are rooted in the belief of one God or creator, prophets versus saints, atoning for sins, when and how to pray, or which religion is the most accurate, when people can't agree, it drives a serious wedge between them and compels them to act and say things that can be disrespectful, hurtful, and even dangerous. Furthermore, when people with differences have not been trained on how to verbally resolve their conflicts, they tend to become more aggressive with their beliefs and behaviors, which is the total opposite of what religion is supposed to represent.

Handling the discussion of sensitive or personal topics requires a level of maturity, decency, courtesy, and respect. Ironically, settling disagreements surrounding the discussion of sensitive or personal topics should use the same character traits. Once we remember that the objective is to walk away from the discussion with our integrity intact, while showing respect to others, then we can honestly say that we are able to properly handle the religious differences among us.

It's common to lose sight of the mission of religious discussions. In some cases, religion is bought up to offer comfort, understanding, insight, and education. Once it's brought up and two people have differing opinions, the conversation goes from comforting to condemning and understanding to shifting blame. These underlying aggressive behaviors are sure to cause conflict. And with any conflict comes the swift and necessary need for a resolution.

It's important for us to realize that a disagreement about a religious discussion should be handled like any other dispute. People come together to determine where the discussion went wrong and how things became so offensive, admit to their contribution to the agreement, and either apologize or agree to disagree. Just because the topic is sensitive does not suggest that people should treat each other with malice. Resolving religious disputes may mean that we should start at the head of religious studies and work our way down. In this instance, it means that we'll have to train our religious leaders how to deal with conflict within their own organization and then they'll be responsible for teaching their members how to settle their differences.

Teaching religious leaders how to resolve religious disputes means showing them how to accept differences, love unconditionally, use discretion, and practice humility. Religious leaders carry a lot of responsibility, as well as a lot of authority. Most of our religious education comes from the words they speak and the practices they encourage us to instill within ourselves and our families. Therefore, if they do not teach acceptance or how to handle religious differences, we'll seldom learn how to do these things, which breeds a society of people who have been taught to condemn another's religion. We should ask and expect our religious leaders to not only teach us the truth and power of our own religion but also how to deal with people who differ from us, regardless of how minor or drastic our differences may be. In addition to teaching us how to do these things, we also need to hold them accountable for practicing what they preach—literally. It is important for our religious leaders to show us how to use diplomacy and respect when talking about another's religion. It is also critical that we see them have conversations with people outside of their religion and deal with the differences in a way that doesn't shed a negative light on the person or their practices. What matters is that we learn, from our religious leaders, that there are many people in the world and even in our community who look, pray, and believe differently than we do, but we have one thing in common—being human. If we can be accepting of that core quality, then we can learn how to resolve disputes based on that common thread alone.

Once our religious leaders are properly trained on how to handle differences, respond to negative speech, and resolve differences, we can expect to see a trickle-down effect, where their knowledge and behaviors pass down to us. We will learn how to communicate differently. And since proper communication is the foundation for dispute resolution, then ultimately, we will resolve our problems effectively. It will start in our churches, pass through our communities and workplaces, and land in our homes. We will eventually make connections between our religious practices and our communication practices. When we become more peaceful and accepting of religious differences, we will also become more peaceful and accepting of each other's general differences.

Differences aside, talking about religion requires strong communication skills overall. Learning how to use your word choice, tone, and ability to use logic and rationalize will be the difference between an intelligent conversation and a heated argument.

Developing this type of communication skill takes time, in addition to resources such as third parties like negotiators, mediators, and arbitrators, especially if the disputes cause organizational or legal problems.

Sometimes religious disputes occur with people who share the same religion but have differences in their opinions. Sometimes the disputes are between people of different cultures who share different practices. Regardless, if we learn how to hear what one another is saying, respect one another's beliefs, and tactfully discuss one another's differences, we could drastically reduce instances of religious disputes that include blaming, shaming, and judging. In all, if we don't take the time to understand the processes of dispute resolution and aren't properly trained on how to use these practices, we'll find ourselves arguing about very sensitive topics that could break relationships or lead to tremendous feuds. And really, when you think about it, religion is the last thing that should sever ties and be used to portray one another in a negative light.

Note from Hez

Violence in America

The United States of American is the most advanced and powerful nation in the world in military preparedness, advanced technology, economics, and standard of living. We are holding our own and can compete globally in every area with a few exceptions: physical and psychological violence. It is the one area where we fall far short, without any strategic plans for improvement. We are fundamentally unable to grasp the essence and root causes of violence, which prohibit us from seeking the appropriate solution or alternatives on how to deal with violence and race relations.

Physical violence, such as assault, rape, or murder, is an extreme form of aggression, the behavior or treatment in which physical force is exerted for the purpose of causing damage or injury.

Psychological violence is anything that an individual or group does to knowingly harm others, be it verbally, mentally, morally, racially, criminally, sexually, or emotionally. It is an act of violence. Psychological violence is by and large rendered with the tongue and time and can be as devastating as physical violence. The physically strongest person can be adversely injured by words.

In fact, gun violence is one of the deadliest components of violence. Approximately ninety individuals are gunned down through gun violence daily, and segregation and discrimination is rampant and appears to be acceptable as a way of life. It is the haves against the have-nots, whites against blacks, rich against poor, male against female, religion against religion, young against old—all listed as a form of violence.

Obviously, there is a reason for our failure in these areas. In my opinion, the basic reason for our failures and the reluctance to address these complex issues is, simply put, economics. In order to address these phenomena, it's going to cost money, which most institutions are unwilling to invest in.

In fact, we have some of the most prestigious colleges and universities in our great country that do an excellent job in preparing students for the world of work. However, we fail miserably in teaching our children how to manage conflict and deal with diversity. We fail to formally teach our children and advanced students how to manage and solve problems beyond the academic criteria. Managing conflict is a skill that can be taught to children and adults. If individuals can learn to solve conflict, it is like learning to swim or ride a bicycle. Once learned, you never forget it. Just think, children are not born violent; violence is a learned behavior, and children by and large become a product of their environment. Children are not born hating others who don't look or worship like them. This hatred is taught to children as they grow up and is passed along from generation to generation by their elders like a rite of passage for no rational reason other than meanness.

This behavior has now spilled over into all segments of our society, even in politics, where it is fashionable to stereotype individuals because of their religion, race, sex, sexual orientation, or nation origin without any consequences, compassion, or feeling for those adversely affected.

In my opinion, one of the methods that are available to address the problem is within our reach due to the seriousness of the issues. I believe that learning the humanistic approach to problem-solving at an early age is essential to our society's success and will ultimately save lives and money. Many of those individuals incarcerated possibly could have avoided incarceration if they were taught some basic skills in learning to resolve conflict, since most children are not equipped with problem-solving skills in the home. Managing conflict and diversity should be a mandatory part of the school curriculum, which will better prepare our children for the real world. To become a holistic person, children need to be taught the importance of self-examination, forgiving, apologizing, having compassion, and developing good listening skills.

Because of the huge problem and the limitation on teachers and administrators in terms of discipline, there must be a different approach. I believe that in order to address this critical problem, every school district should implement a mandatory conflict resolution training program in K-12, recognizing that there is a cost factor involved. I further believe that this recommendation is not the ultimate panacea, but if implemented, it will pay tremendous dividends and ultimately save lives and money, and in some instances, prevent incarceration.

Anger Management

ADDRESSING TECHNIQUES ON MANAGING ANGER

In writing this chapter, there were numerous approaches to addressing anger and what individuals do when they get angry. The following are some of the responses: cry, pray, exercise, clean, stop communications, curse, talk to spiritual leaders, talk to friends, shut down, wish that the opposing party was dead, mentally argue, plan to get the individual(s) back, go for a walk, go for a drive, drink alcohol, do drugs. Some admitted that they were unaware or simply did not remember what they did when they became angry.

It must be pointed out that there are a variety of things that one can do to avoid violence. One must avoid violence at all cost. Violent behavior, whether provoked or self-initiated, is an outward emotional expression of anger. When one is driven to physically assault another person, we assume that this person has no control over their emotions. This is only a part of the problem. A more deeply disturbing issue is that their violence is due to an inability to verbally express themselves and communicate their emotions. A person who commits violent acts may not have been introduced to effective communication. In fact, we were invited to Rikers Island Prison Complex in New York City to do a session on anger management for the inmates. After the session, one of the inmates came over to me and thanked us for the presentation. In addition, he informed us that he appreciated the anger management training and stated that if he and other inmates had been exposed to this type of training, some of them would not have been incarcerated. He further stated that the individual he was involved in the altercation with "dissed" (disrespected) him, and he killed him. He was serving a life sentence.

Of all the human emotions society experiences daily, anger is the most powerful and poorly managed feeling. Although anger is considered to be a healthy normal human emotion, it varies in intensity from mild irritation to intense fury and rage. It can take control and become destructive, leading to intense fury and rage. It can take control and become destructive, leading to problems at home, at work, and in one's personal life, as well as jeopardizing the quality of your life. In fact, anger is a stronger feeling than love and can have a devastating impact on the individual who is incapable of controlling their anger. Anger impacts the individual who is angry more than it impacts the individual(s) they are angry with. In fact, if you are angry at another individual, every time you encounter or are in the presence of that person, you get angry again.

People have varying opinions, beliefs, and ideas. Additionally, people express themselves in different styles, ranging from shifts in body language to the pitch or harshness of their voices. When they are angry, frustrated, or feeling any other negative emotion, these expressions can come out in a multitude of ways. One way that it shouldn't reveal itself is through violence. Violence does not fully express a person's emotions. In fact, it only showcases one emotion, which is rage. Violence doesn't necessarily let another person know that some are hurt, embarrassed, overwhelmed, and feeling misunderstood or otherwise emotionally distraught. It just shows the highest level of anger, which becomes rage.

When people learn how to express the full range of their emotions without using rage, they'll find that they can express themselves more clearly. They'll also find that others become more receptive of their emotions and will become more eager to resolve any negativity that is causing such hardship. The open communication about negative emotions leads to quicker and more supportive conflict resolution. If two or more people can learn how to explain their differences, express how it makes them feel, and then have the desire to work things out, it encourages a problem-solving environment. Eventually, after enough talking, whether through mediation or arbitration, all parties will feel as though they've had ample opportunities to express themselves, and the threat of violence is virtually eliminated.

There's an important first step that we must take to learn how to thwart violent behavior, and that step is to understand our anger: what triggers it, how to deal with it, and how to communicate it to others.

As a mediator and arbitrator, I've seen my fair share of hostile environments. I've been in boardrooms where people are ready to go at each other's throats. I've been in factories where workers looked as if they'd use a piece of machinery as a weapon. In all cases, the imminent threat of rage wasn't coming from career criminals and killers. There were everyday people who had reached a tipping point with their anger and frustration. For them, words weren't powerful enough to express how betrayed and fearful they were. There wasn't a vocabulary word large enough to describe how livid they were with another person. The threat of rage and violence wasn't premeditated. It was due to a lack of understanding on how to express their version of the story and all the emotional details. They couldn't battle with their words and use facts to back them up. To them, it would be much easier to find a weapon or use their hands to alleviate their aggression and address their emotional despair. Violence was the likely answer.

We see it all the time in the news. People engage in street fights, domestic violence, bar brawls, and shoving and pushing because the level of their anger is too large for words. It's not because the words don't exist. It's not because the people aren't smart enough to use them. These violent behaviors happen because they may not have been introduced to communication and conflict resolution. So when they are triggered, regardless of how small or insignificant the trigger may be, they respond with their fists, a gun, or any other weapon of choice.

Our society begets violence. We move at such a frantic pace that our patience has decreased while our erratic behaviors have increased. Everything frustrates us—traffic, the wrong coffee order at the local coffee shop, glitches in our technology, and anything that is remotely inconvenient. Instead of slowing down to process information, we demand that everything moves faster while making our lives easier.

The students being educated within our school system are constantly engaged in or made aware of violence. Whether it's in the schoolyard, classroom, or on the way to and from school, children are exposed to violence as a way of communicating their personality or defending the things that matter to them. Their fragile minds aren't processing better ways to manage their anger, defend themselves, or express their feelings. They participate in irrational cause-and-effect behaviors, where the slightest aggression is the cause and the violent behavior is the effect.

Regardless of age or profession, violent behavior is a serious problem. Seemingly, we're using brawn over brain to solve our menial and significant problems. There doesn't seem to be a filter that helps people sort what needs to be handled with communication, walking away, or otherwise diffusing the situation. Instead people seem to have their finger hovering over the button that activates their violent tendencies, and the slightest disagreement is enough to make them push the button and shift into gear.

As I've mentioned, in being in a professional setting, you would think that the more education one has or the more money one makes, the less likely they are to participate in a battle of the brawn. However, factors such as education or income do not cause one to be less susceptible to anger. To understand how we can alleviate violence, we must understand what angers us and how to deal with the raw emotion of anger.

First and foremost, anger is a normal emotion. As humans, we have a dichotomy of emotions that range from love to hate, happiness to sadness, and peacefulness to anger. We must accept that anger is an emotion that exists within us, but it does not have to take over us or control our behaviors. Our anger tells us that something has not settled well with our mind and heart. It is that uncomfortable feeling when you cannot seem to process your emotions quick enough to respond in a dignified manner. Anger only becomes an issue when it is not able to be controlled.

Anger is not something that sneaks up on us. We do not snap, like the Incredible Hulk, and begin to terrorize anything within our path. It usually builds up. However, we receive several warning signals that we are becoming angry. People who respond with violent behavior usually ignore all the signs, either because they would rather respond with anger or because they do not know how to recognize what is going on. Initially, we feel it in our body, when our temperature changes and we become more rigid in response to our feelings of disappointment, irritation, and hurt. Then our words become sharper and less substantial, yet they are meaner and more direct. We use our words as the first point of violent contact and then back it up with physical contact. This process can be a matter of moments or can be built up over a longer period. Regardless, once anger has been triggered, there are only a few ways to deal with it: talk about it, suppress it, or act upon it. Talking through our issues is the best step to take. It has the least detrimental effects, although it takes the most amount of maturity and the most patience.

When I act as a mediator or arbitrator who is negotiating the toughest of terms and issues, I am constantly reminding people that having a third party to help settle their problems is not a weakness. When people feel as if they are weak, unable to rationalize their emotions, or incapable of resolving their own problems, they want to respond in ways that make them feel like they are in control. Usually, this creates a violent situation. Oftentimes, bruised egos and inappropriate communication creates huge barriers in resolving a problem. My job is to teach people how to avoid that by putting their egos to rest and using their words more constructively.

Resolving conflict must be, most importantly, a desire. The people who are on the verge of physically acting out their emotions must want to find another way to handle things. Even more meaningful, these people must be surrounded by another person or other people who want to see them handle things differently. Things tend to get out of hand when a crowd is around and is encouraging negative behavior. To solve a problem, you must be in the midst of problem solvers.

However, at the core, anger must be managed by the person who is angry. No one person can manage another person's anger. They can subdue it and try to talk sense into the person, but in the end, that person must want to calm down and handle things appropriately. Violence is not the answer for resolving a problem. In fact, it simply creates bigger and more complicated problems. There is nothing to be gained by reacting with violence. No one person benefits from violence, but many people can be hurt by it.

In processing anger, as an attempt to avoid violence and become a better communicator, it is important to remember a few things.

First, understand and recognize your anger. It is important to know what your triggers are and when those triggers have been engaged and activated. Second, learn how to calm down. Stepping away from the situation or surrounding yourself with people who do not want you to (or will not allow you to) respond negatively will give you a reality check and likely, a source of reason. Next, try to understand the situation a bit better. Think about what has brought you to this tipping point and how you would like to change things. Evaluate if this situation is worth the attention, and if it is worth the attention, how you can possibly address it more rationally.

Then talk to the other person. Find a neutral place where you can talk about the underlying issues that are affecting the both of you. Approach this meeting with open-mindedness, a willingness to hear their side of the story, as well as express your feelings, opinions, and ideas. The "meeting of the minds" may not immediately resolve the problem. You may have to meet several times, but keep going until you both agree to amicably end the discussion or accept each other's differences.

Resolving your conflicts by using effective communication, third-party assistance, and rationale will help you avoid violent situations. However, if you find that another person refuses to back down from their violent acts, remember to use your common sense by protecting yourself, seeking qualified and appropriate help, and staying safe.

18 Ways People Tend to React When They Get Angry

Anger is a stronger feeling than love and can have a devastating impact on the individual who is unable to control their anger.

To learn to control anger, one must be taught the stages of anger. Anger impacts the individual who is angry more than it impacts the individual(s) they are angry with. For example, if you are angry at an individual, every time you are in their presence, it affects you. Therefore, it is incumbent on you to seek a solution to the problem.

How do you respond to anger? How have you seen others respond to their anger? Here is a list of common responses to anger. Once you read the list, see if you can determine if any of these responses are conducive to resolving a problem. If not, what can be done better?

1. Cry.

2. Pray.

3. Exercise.

4. Clean.

5. Stop communicating.

6. Call names; curse.

7. Talk to spiritual leaders.

8. Talk to friends.

9. Shut down.

10. Get violent.

11. Wish that the opposing party was dead.

12. Mentally argue.

13. Plan to get the individual(s) back.

14. Go for a walk.

15. Get in the car and go for a drive.

16. Use drugs and alcohol.

17. Text, e-mail, Facebook, Instagram, Twitter, and others.

18. In many instances, individuals simply don't know or remember what they do when they become angry.

Understanding Conflict

According to *Webster's Dictionary*, conflict is "a fight, struggle, or battle: a disagreement, dispute, or a quarrel." Conflict can also be defined as a sharp disagreement or collision in interests, ideas, etc.

Individuals deal with conflict in different ways. Some refuse to admit that it exists, while others blame themselves. Therefore, it is important to understand the methods and processes used to resolve conflict. Those processes are call alternative dispute resolution (ADR), negotiations, mediation, arbitration, and fact-finding.

A Quick Review of Conflict Management

- Acknowledge that it is okay to disagree.

- Acknowledge the emotional issues.

- Listen actively.

- Identify areas of agreement.

- Clarify the differences of opinion—rely on the facts.

- Discuss the value of different viewpoints.

- Understand the differences and the reasons for them.

- Put yourself in the other person's position.

- Be open-minded.

- Use problem-solving.

- Generate many potential solutions.

- Try to extract the best attributes of each conflicting idea.

- Keep the conflict focused on opinions and facts, not people.

The Traits of Successful People

Conflicted relationships tend to have two main parts: assumptions and assumptions that lead to negative outcomes.

Negative Outcomes (Based on Assumptions)

- One-sided victories

- Compromise

- High stakes and cost to both parties

- Neither party fully achieves goals—joint gains unrealized

- Slow decay and decline of both parties

- Escalation to rapid destruction

Things as small as arguments and things as large as wars are all types of conflict. Conflict is a natural part of our lives and occurs whenever people live, work, or play together. Unfortunately, not enough time is spent learning about the causes and consequences of conflict, and even less time is spent learning how to resolve it.

People do live, work, and play together, so conflict is inevitable. However, how can we become successful at managing conflict and increasing the number of positive outcomes in our lives?

Turning Conflict into Success

Successful people can manage their adversities and discrepancies very well. Here are some traits that you can learn and adapt to increase the success in your life.

- Understand yourself and how your behavior affects others.

- Understand your reactions to other people.

- Know how to maximize what you do.

- Have a positive attitude about yourself, which will cause other to have confidence in themselves.

- Know how to adapt your behavior to meet the needs of other people and particular situations.

Relationship by Objective—RBO

Prior to joining the Cornell University staff as the director of labor-management programs, I was employed by the Federal Mediation & Conciliation Service[2] as a commissioner. My primary responsibilities as a federal mediator were to mediate disputes and give technical assistance when needed.

In my twelve years as a federal mediator, I primarily mediated disputes between labor and management in the northeastern part of the United States, including Puerto Rico and the Virgin Islands. One of the special and unique services provided by The Federal Mediation and Conciliation Service was the preventive, proactive technical services to avoid major strikes and shutdowns and improve the relationship between labor and management. If there was a prolonged strike or a detection of poor communication and mistrust between the parties, which led to a poor day-to-day relationship, mediators would assist the parties by providing a free service to the parties. Mediator was well equipped to assist the parties by establishing labor-management committees, or in some instances, providing relationship by objective programs. The relationship by objective program (RBO) provided a more in-depth two- to three-day retreat program away from the work site where the parties

[2] The Federal Mediation and Conciliation Service, created in 1947, is an independent agency whose mission is to preserve and promote labor-management peace and cooperation. Headquartered in Washington, DC, with ten regional offices and more than sixty field offices, the agency provides mediation and conflict resolution services to industry, government agencies, and communities.

were required to stay on the designated premises throughout the program to deal with attitudes and practices and learn how to solve problems at all levels of management and unions. This process was designed by the Federal Mediation & Conciliation Service, through commissioners John Popular and Jerry Barrett. The key to the success of the RBO is the fact that employees and management define and identify their own problems. They analyze those problems and then establish goals in order to overcome those problems. They formulate specific action steps to meet those goals. Last, they set their own timetable and assign individuals to each step to assure that the goals are implemented.

In defining the goals, the parties jointly define the elements of a poor employee-management relationship such as

- Mistrust

- Animosity

- Lawsuits

- Poor communication

- Excessive discipline

- Numerous arbitrations

Throughout the RBO process, employees and management will find themselves meeting in three different forms of groups. With tasks and assignments given to each group at various phases of the RBO, the group interchanged and utilized so as to maximize the ideas of all participants.

During the process, the joint groups agree on specific mutual objectives such as the following:

- Training

- Communication

- Attitudes and practices / employees

- Attitudes and practices / administration

- Employee-management relations
- Others

Task: Develop actions, steps, and recommendations to accomplish objectives of team categories.

This RBO process is one of the most effective, innovative, and creative programs because everyone is encouraged to participate and offer them input during the entire process.

In addition, there were mandatory trainings that all participants had to participate in during this process. The trainings are as follows:

- Anger management
- Conflict resolution
- Dealing with difficult people
- Developing good listening skills
- Managing change
- Problem-solving
- Team building

After participating in hundreds of these types of effective workshops, it influenced me to replicate these procedures outside of the labor-management communities and into communities like Board of Education, Non-Profit Board of Directors, and other institutions. The process worked at a higher degree outside of the labor-management community. The reason for the success of the RBO process is that everyone receives the same training and are able to make positive recommendations, which translate into taking ownership.

Resources

CONFLICT RESOLUTION TERMINOLOGY

The terminology used in conflict resolution means different things to different people. Sometimes people may not even explicitly define a situation as a conflict or dispute—they may simply talk about "hassles," "disagreements," or the need to "make a decision on a controversial issue."

People also deal with conflict in many ways. They may pretend it doesn't exist or give in without a fight, they may try to cool the situation off by resolving the obvious problem without addressing the issues that caused it in the first place, or they may confront it head-on.

In confronting conflict, some rely on violence or power to impose a solution. Others sit down—formally or informally—and attempt to cooperatively work out their problems through *negotiation*, sometimes getting the help of a *mediator*. They may also use a *fact finder* or agree to refer the issues to an *arbitrator* for a final and binding decision.

Negotiation is a process by which those in conflict try to agree on a mutually acceptable way to handle their differences. It can be used to address differences within groups, as well as between and among groups or individuals. It involves a willingness to be flexible and compromise and generally involves direct discussions between the disputing parties. Sometimes, however, those engaged in negotiation need help to make the process work.

Mediation may provide the help that will enable people or groups in conflict to reach an agreement. It is used by people who have reached an impasse in negotiations and by people who can't even begin talking to each other. It involves using an individual(s) or group(s) acceptable to the parties as an intermediary. However, the parties to the dispute retain the decision-making power.

Fact-finding is a process by which a person or panel of persons, who are not involved in the dispute, comply and report facts and differing perception of facts. The fact finder's report may then be used to develop a framework both parties can use as a basis for discussion, negotiation, or settlement. This process may involve formal hearings, informal hearings, interviews, and/or research. Sometimes fact finders make specific recommendations for settlement. As in mediation, it leaves the decision-making power with the parties to the dispute.

Arbitration is used when the parties agree to let an impartial third party decide for them, and then agree to be bound by the decision. Unlike the other processes, arbitration takes the power to decide from the disputing parties.

Although fact-finding and arbitration are important components of the conflict resolution system, they are beyond the scope of the manual.

Some people or organizations set up systems to deal with conflict when it arises, while others approach conflict resolution on an ad hoc, unplanned basis.

Barriers to Resolving Conflict

- Anger
- Ego
- Lack of formal training in resolving disputes
- Poor listening skills
- Heresy
- Body language
- Unwillingness to accept facts
- Reluctance to admit wrongdoing
- Pigheadedness
- Attitude
- Strong family beliefs
- Culture
- Frustration
- Hostility
- A closed mind
- Reluctance to accept change
- Self-centeredness

We Can't Legislate Attitudes

The recent mood of some individuals and groups in our Country regarding the recent killing of 9 individuals at Bible study, and the activity of the Supreme Court, the United State Congress including the North Carolina Legislature has convinced me and others that it is impossible to legislate attitudes, racial harmony and tolerance.

The question before the American Public is "Have we truly made progress?" We are quick to state African Americans have made an enormous amount of progress. We are slow to acknowledge the constant presence of "Jim Crow", as many of the advances are "legislated away".

It is amazing, that in 2015, African Americans, who are embedded in the underlying fabric of the economic and cultural success of the United States of America, continue to suffer from various forms of degradation and inequality. The Supreme Court's recent decision helps us clearly understand that the preamble to the Constitution, ("we the people"...) still does not mean "us".

We have attempted to legislate racial attitudes and social justice since the 19th Century in America; beginning with the Plessey vs. Ferguson decision where the Supreme Court ruled that the Separate but Equal Doctrine was Constitutional. The decision promoted further division.

These attempts at legislating attitudes continued with the Thirteenth Amendment, to the Constitution, which prohibits slavery; The Fourteenth Amendment, which guarantees equal protection under the law; the Fifteenth Amendment that forbid discrimination in access to voting; and President Roosevelt signed executive Order 8802 which outlawed Segregationist hiring policies for Federal Defense Contracts, In addition, in 1953, President Truman urged the Bureau of Employment Security to implement the policy of non-discrimination; The 1957 Civil Rights Act, The 1960 Civil Rights Act, In 1961, President Kennedy issued Executive Order 10925, which required Federal Contractors to take Affirmative Action that addressed how employees were treated during employment; The same language was used in President Johnson's Executive Order 11246; The 1964 Civil Rights Act of 1964 which again prohibited employment discrimination; The Fair Housing Laws of 1964, The 1965 Voting rights Act; The Civil Rights Act of 1966, again was designed to protect persons from discrimination and the list continues.

In essence, all of the above legislation was passed in good faith addressing the attitudes of a minority of individuals toward African Americans in regards to equal employment, housing, voting rights and basic civil rights. However, the one thing that was missing is, how to implement and change the attitude and how individual feel and treat one another who are different. Therefore, in order to address the growing problem, all races must accept the fact that children are not born hating, and disliking other races because of the color of their skin or because they are different. This whole issue of racism is hereditary and is continuously passed on from generation to generation in a clandestine "right's of passage" philosophy without any consequences. Therefore, since we are unable to legislature, attitudes, let's work together and address the issues that separate us in an intelligent and non threatening manner. We are all Americans.

We should learn to love our youth before they are involved in the Criminal justice system

Several years ago I was asked to speak to a group of African American Youth about turning their lives around and becoming good law abiding citizens. I stressed the importance of education, employment, self-esteem, fatherhood and family values. Incidentally, many of the youth in this group had been labeled incorrigible and some had been in the criminal justice system for years. As I started to talk to this group, I noticed a sense of insecurities, and "a lack of interest". I could see that I was not getting across to these young men. I then changed my approach and started to question them about their future, family, fatherhood and their long term interest. That question created the beginning of a long and serious dialogue. Incidentally, a large number of the youth lived in single family homes, some lived in shelters and other did not have a place called home. As the dialogue advanced, I was informed by these individuals that they were doomed for life because, they had committed felonies and would be ineligible to get a good paying job. Even after serving their time they are still being punished for the same crime. In fact one of the individuals referred to the felony sentence as a life sentence that forced individuals into a lifetime of second class citizenship. They expressed to me that they were not going to subscribe to second class citizenship under any circumstances. Again, they were pretty adamant about their positions and showed no signs or caring about the long term consequences or valued life as most of us know it. Many of them stated that they knew that they were going to die before they reached the age of 25, so be it. In fact, most of them had the same philosophy! If they completed their education, it would not change their status or contribute to them getting a good paying job because of their label. Therefore, in their opinion, they felt they were relegated to a life of gangs, drug dealing, burglary and other forms of crime due to the standards set by society.

I shared my work experience and the importance of being good law abiding citizens with this group of young men. I further stressed the pitfalls and detriments becoming a professional criminal who got caught up in our criminal injustice system. A large number of individuals are incarcerated for low level crimes and truly receive a life sentence once a felony is committed. Many believe that in order to solve these problems, the solution would be to build more jails and lock them up. Obviously, that trend of thinking is not working because those who are incarcerated serve time and return back to society without any skills and in too many instances resort to crime in order to survive.

As many know, we are dealing with a serious phenomenon without any long term solutions. It is my belief that if we are going to solve a problem, we must first define the problem. After defining the problem, we must seek rational reasonable and doable solutions to address the specific problem. If we define the wrong problem, we will certainly create the wrong solution. In this instance, the fact is many of those individuals who have given up on life and are not afraid of dying or killing others or going to jail is a problem that needs to be addressed. In my opinion, we recently witnessed some of those youngsters where approximately 50 individuals were killed in Chicago. In Baltimore, 40 individuals were killed in one month. I believe that many of those involved in these shootings fit the profile of that group of young men I met with who had given up on life. When one gives up on their own life, they do not value others' life.

We must address the issue of the life time sentencing that prohibits some individuals who could be rehabilitated and becoming model citizens if given the right opportunity. In addition, we must encourage the correctional institutions to offer survival and life skills that individuals could use as they return to society. We must re-educate those individuals by offering Vocational Programs while they are incarcerated so they have skills to survive. In most instances, if individuals have vocational skills such as painters, plumbers, electricians, landscapers, brick masons, carpenter, auto mechanic, computer repairmen, chef, etc. they have the opportunity to fill a void instead of seeking employment where they would be rejected due to their criminal background.

There are a number of initiatives that we must take to address these problems similar to what was written in an article by Columnist Bob Herbert. He wrote that "it is inconceivable in this atmosphere that blacks themselves will not mobilize in a major way to save the young people. If we continue to stand by and wait on Government to deal with the problems haunting the Black community, we are doomed and in the same boat as those who have given up on life." I firmly believe that we must use a multitude of approaches and strategies including engaging the entire community and stakeholders.

Moreover, the issues that we are faced with simply cannot wait until the next young person is killed and the individual who killed him is arrested, and we dust off our protest boots and march for justice. We must join together and create a dialogue with all parties that could potentially be affected: and start to address the issues at hand and collectively seek reasonable approaches to these systemic problems. In addition, those communities who are not facing the same kind of issues regarding violence must be proactive and start to address these issues before the crises arrive. We must create credible programs that can be replicated in other areas that will give some of those who have given up on life a better vision and assure them that we care.

Hezekiah Brown
Elizabeth City, North Carolina

THE WAR IS HERE AND BLACK LIVES MATTER

A s I read the Newspaper and watch television, I continue to see information stating that "BLACK LIVES MATTER". I am in full agreement that Black Lives does matter. The part that is quite confusing and contradictory is when does Black Lives matter? Does it only matter when a white policeman pull the trigger or is it equally as devastating when a black youth is gunned down by another black. It is apparent to me that Black Lives only matter to some when it involves a person or opposite color or culture who is involved in the killing. I firmly believe that if we are sincere when we say Black Lives matter, then it shouldn't matter who pulled the trigger, be it black or white.

Moreover, I am gravely concerned about the excessive number of Africans Americans who are being gunned down on the streets of America by both, Law Enforcement and Gang Related or others.

The unadulterated crime of this all is the enormous amount of young African American males who are being gunned down on a daily basis by other African Americans. The irony of all of this black on black crime almost go unnoticed, without any loud outcry or protest from the powers to be including, some of the prominent Institutions who have the authority and ability to make a difference.

When an African American is killed by a white policeman, hundreds and thousands of individuals gather and demonstrate and demand accountability. However, when an African American is gunned down by another African American, there aren't any demonstrations or demand for accountability, it just business as usual which lead me to ask the question again. Dose Black really matter".

I am further appalled at the notion that there is not a single day that pass without breaking news informing the general public that someone has been gunned down at our Colleges and Universities, Military Institutions, Communities, Shopping Malls and even on the job throughout the United States. In fact, we have lost more African Americans on our streets in the United States than we lost in the Iraq and Afghanistan wars on terror. In the 10 to 12 year "war on terror" in Afghanistan and Iraq which was one of the most sophisticated and technological wars, in modern time. Approximately 12,000 soldiers were killed. On the other hand in that same period of time, we lost approximately 25,000 African Americans per year, to gang related and others. That 12 year total equals approximately 250.000 African Americans over that same period that unnecessarily died at the hands of other African Americans without demonstrations, investigations or special prosecutors.

I believe that the situation is so severe that it has earned the term epidemic and it is not just a problem for African Americans because epidemics don't stop in one City or State, it spreads to all communities, America can no longer sit idly by and let this disastrous detrimental activity take place. If we can spend billions of dollars on ☻ wars in places like Afghanistan, Iraq Egypt and other Countries, we should be willing to invest in this epidemic at home. It is time for America to address this epidemic with the same vigor and energy that we address matters in other Countries because this crime has serious consequences that perpetrates itself in the following manner.

Most of those young men who are involved in gang wars and are killed, or incarcerated leaving thousands of children fatherless and consequently to single female parent which ultimately end up creating an enormous economic burden on society. Keep in mind that the cost to house one inmate cost a minimum of $25,000 plus the cost of feeding, housing and educating those children left behind. I conclude by asking the rhetorical question. Does Black Lives Really Matter?

Loud Few Urge Strife to Keep the Silent Majority Divided

After having conversation with a diverse group of individuals across the Country regarding the current situation we are facing in America regarding the recent shooting of two New York City Policemen, the shooting of Michael Brown by a police in Ferguson, Missouri, and the death of Eric Garner at the hands of a police in Staten Island, New York, we have come to several conclusions. The first is that we are moving more toward a racial divided Country and it is due to the small percentage of individuals who are experts at creating problems and the politicians who take advantage of those situations by playing the blame game. As an example of the latter, I refer you to the statement made by Former Mayor Rudolph Giuliani. He stated that President Obama is to blame for the two policemen who were killed in NYC. He went on to say that President Obama had engaged in propaganda encouraging people to hate Policemen. Others blamed Attorney General, Eric Holder for the Officers' death. This accusation is far from the truth. However, it sounds good to a few who insist on further perpetuating this racial divisiveness by falsely accusing two Africans American who hold high positions and blame them for the killing of the two New York City Policemen. In addition, it waves the flag for those hypocrite who would entertain this type of hypocrisy.

In my opinion, blaming President Obama and Attorney General Holder is not going to solve the problems because the vast majority of Americans know that they are not the problem regarding the issues between Law Enforcement and the Minority Communities.

We further concluded that there is an inordinate amount of covert bias on the part of both blacks and whites that is surfacing amongst all races while the silent majority remains silent. Individuals feel that they must take a position along racial lines on the Ferguson, Missouri and Staten Island, New York conflict, others feels that they must take a position on the killing of two New York City Policemen and using it to further divide the Country along racial lines. In taking this position, they are by and large taken along racial lines which complicate the matter even more. In most instances, many whites believe that the policemen were justified in their action. On the other hand most blacks believe that the action taken by the policemen was not justified. However, one of the things we all agree upon is that the fatal shooting of policemen Rafael Ramos and Wenjian Liu was not justified. We further agree that this shooting was done by a lone deranged, mentally unstable young man who happened to be black. Ismaaiyl Brinsley shot his girlfriend, who was African American, and subsequently killed an Asian and Hispanic policeman, which clearly indicated that his actions were, not racially motivated and we should not be media hyped into believing that race was a factor. He was a dangerous individual who ultimately took his own life which further confirmed that he was unstable. Therefore, the American Public nor Law Enforcement should not use this isolated incident as a measuring tool in making a determination or passing judgment on the Minority Community and Law Enforcement, nor should the Politicians use this incident as a tool to promote the 2016 election. This is a serious matter and has to be addressed by all Americans, because it is affecting all Americans. We must first figure out what the real problem is and proceed to seeking mutual solutions to the real problems. Incidentally, if we define the wrong problem, we will obviously come up with the wrong solution.

These negative conversations regarding the relationship between Law Enforcement and the Minority community are taking place in the work place, religious community and the community at large based on information they receive from the news media which further exacerbates the problems. In my conversation, most all agreed that the issue that drives the situations is driven by the behavior of a small percentage of the Law Enforcement and the Minority Community. However, the real issue that is before the American Public is what we should do about this self-destructive problem that has the tendency to tear our Country apart.

All I hear is we need to start a conversation about the issues. For Christ Sake, when are we going to do it? After another individual(s) is killed.

Hezekiah Brown
Elizabeth City, NC

Ultra Conservatives advocate for reducing extended unemployment benefits because if they receive unemployment benefits for an extended period of time, they are reluctant to seek other jobs. On the other hand, Legislators are voting to increase sales taxes on food, energy, property taxes while the market value of homes continue to decline, increase in college tuition, clothing, water, etc.

Ultra conservatives believe that the answer to the problem in Public education is increasing the amount of charter schools and providing funds for private and religious schools.

The Dilemma of Circumstances and Reality in Student Loans

The old adage that a picture says a thousand words became a reality to me when I recently saw a cartoon in the newspaper which displayed a recent college graduate sitting on a big rock in his cap and gown. Under his gown was a huge rock entitled "DEBT". On the side of the huge rock was the college student parents who stated "THERE'S

OUR BIG COLLEGE GRAD LOOK HOW MUCH HE'S GROWN." The inference was that he had grown educationally as well as created a huge debt that would have to be repaid over a period of time. What are the consequences and reality of this young person and thousands of other who are in the same boat?

Many young people are informed at a very early age that the way out of poverty and the route to the middle and upper class is education. We stress the importance of education and constantly encourage our young population to attend College regardless of the cost. That philosophy works for many youth if they are not trapped by circumstances and reality regarding student loans. The circumstances are real and the consequences are unforeseen when a young person is receiving a student loan. In reality, students do not connect the dots in terms of the dire consequences and subsequent impact of the student loan. In funding their education through a student loan, they are led to believe that this is the route to the American Dream. Little do they know that after completing their college degree a Bachelor, Master or PhD, reality sit in and the circumstances drastically change. In many instances in order to acquire these degrees, they must by and large mortgage a large portion of their early life to repay the student loan. In fact, the loans could amount anywhere from $75,000 to $100,000 or more, that's when reality set in again. Then, there is a strong possibility that the circumstances could change if they meet someone while in college and they decide to get married with the identical student loan obligations. This couple could very well be in debt for almost $200,000 without employment. Subsequently they land jobs earning anywhere from $25,000 to $60,000 per year with an enormous student loan debt to repay. Thereafter, it becomes apparent that they cannot meet their obligation in repaying the loan due to the huge financial obligation created by reality and circumstances. These unforeseen circumstances force the individuals to default on the student loans not realizing the ultimate impact of defaulting on the loan. The reality becomes factual by virtue of the cost of the monthly obligation of repaying the loan. The monthly payment could very well exceed $1,000.00 per month. The reality is real, if an individual default on a student loan, they are automatically prohibited from attaining a FHA mortgage and their credit rating is severely damages for several years which have other negative implications. Bad credit has far reaching negative circumstances which can affect job promotions and prohibit individuals from attaining employment with major companies. In the event those same two individuals subsequently opt to seek other employment, reality raises it head again and because of a poor credit rating, they are prohibited from acquiring a better job.

Therefore, it is incumbent upon parents/guardians to seek other rational methods of supplementing the huge cost of education prior to students graduating from high school.

There are numerous other alternatives available to pay for education other than through student loans. Parents/guardians can purchase whole life insurance at an early age or seek special college tuition pro-grams offered by banks or investment companies including grants in order to reduce the enormous cost of student loans.

We can do better.

Hezekiah Brown
Elizabeth City

Gun Violence in America

As we mourn the shooting of 102 individuals of which 53 survived in Orlando, Florida by an individual who has been label as a closet gay wannabee, a gay sympathizer, terrorist, wife abuser, ISSIS supporter, Muslim and many other names, the labeling doesn't ease the pain for the surviving families.

We continue to mourn the cruel death of the Charleston "9" who was gunned down while attending Bible study in the Church by another deranged individual whose goal was to start a race war. Over the July 4, 2016 weekend, 4 individuals were killed and 58 wounded in Chicago, Illinois. In addition, 5 policemen were killed and 6 wounded in Texas, 2 individual killed by policemen 1 in Louisiana, another in Minnesota and 300 individuals arrested and numerous policemen injured at peaceful demonstrations. If you watch Virginia television, almost every day, there are multiple shootings as well as other cities in the United States.

We are also reminded of the continued gun violence existence that take the lives of young and old people overall, averaging approximately 90 per day, including some as young as 6 months old. In fact, there were approximately 355 mass shooting in 336 days in 2015 without any comprehensive proactive or preventive programs aimed at taking a realistic approach to addressing this devastating phenomena.

Communities invest millions of dollars in body cameras for policemen; School Districts invest millions of dollars in metal detectors and cameras. Communities also spend huge sums of money on purchasing community cameras to observe crime as it is being committed, including hiring more policemen.

In my opinion, some of the above processes are absolutely essential in apprehending the criminals after they have committed a crime. However, we, they are reluctant to invest in any proactive measures such as dealing with the root causes of these deadly incidents. Building more Correctional Institutions for incarceration is not the panacea because the recidivism rate exceeds 65%. That means that approximately 65% of individuals who commit crime and is ultimately incarcerated ends up returning to jail which means that this system is also failing. Proactive and preventive programs simply do not exist to the degree that is warranted. Programs for some of these disturbed individuals are being cut from budget all across the nation in order to save money. Those closed minded attitudes must change.

It is time for us to seek reasonable alternatives to address this situation by identifying and addressing the real problem. For example, we know that when an individual is stopped by a policeman for violating the law for speeding, broken tail light or other car malfunction, in many instances they are angry at themselves and the policeman which set up a scenario that puts them both at risk. I am suggesting that since we have witnessed most of this scenario, it is time to deal with the humanistic and common sense approach to addressing this problem. In my opinion, there should be dialogue taking place all across the Country where individuals are seeking a methodology that would prevent the policeman in specific cases from ever having to leave their car. In the age of advanced technology, and a climate conducive to problem solving, policemen, community members and technology experts could examine some of the cases that have seriously injured policemen and individuals and seek a reasonable solution to address this phenomena. Maybe through technology, a policeman could get the information they need concerning driver license and car registration without having to come face to face with a potential criminal. In this case scenario I described, if an individual refuses to comply through technology, the policeman would have the ability to call for back-up which will create a cooling off period and not put anyone's life at risk. In addition, policemen/ policewomen, families, community organizations, religious and educational institutions will have to do their part in teaching and training our youth/policemen on "how to react" when these deadly circumstance surface. We become experts at defining the problems and short on seeking rational solutions.

It is my belief that we are never going to solve these issues until we change our attitude, practices and approaches and be serious and do what is necessary to address the issues that create these problems. We are not going to solve the problems by using power to combat power. We need to invest in people because they are the root of the problems. We have to teach individuals how to problem solve by starting at the earliest age and continue through High School and College, including the workplace, recognizing that there is a cost factor. We must invest in programs for emotionally disturbed individuals instead of hiring more policemen or building more jails. I am convinced that hiring more policemen, passing more legislation, throwing out elected and appointed officials, is like putting a Band-Aid on a big cut. We need to add the humanistic approach to all of the above approaches where individual learn how to deal with anger, stress, daily challenges, change, trust, respect for themselves and others, family values and personal conflicts. That is the humanistic component where individuals are taught the necessary skills in resolving disputes instead of destroying each other.

We can do better.

Hezekiah Brown
Elizabeth City, North Carolina

References

Brown, A. A. 2012. *Techniques & Strategies: To Increase Parent Involvement.* Bloomington, Indiana: Xlibris.

Brown, A. A. 2013. *Parent Engagement Effects Student Drop Out.*

Bloomington, Indiana: Author House.

Brown, Brown & Associates Conflict Resolution Center.

Brown, Hezekiah. "Conflict Resolution in Classrooms Could Curb Violence" *The Daily Advance* June 26, 2016.

Bush, R. A. B. & Folger, J. P. 2004. *The Promise of Mediation: The Transformative Approach to Conflict.* San Francisco, California: Jossey-Bass.

Constantino, C. A. & Merchant, C. S. 1995. *Designing Conflict Management Systems: A Guide to Creating Productive and Healthy Organizations.* San Francisco, California: Jossey-Bass.

Harvard Business School Press. 2008. *Managing Difficult Interactions: Expert Solutions to Everyday Challenges.* Brighton, Massachusetts. Harvard Business School Press.

Kheel, T. W. 1999. *The Keys to Conflict Resolution: Proven Methods of Resolving Disputes.* New York, New York: Four Walls Eight Windows.

Kottler, J. A. 1996. *Beyond Blame: A New Way of Resolving Conflicts in Relationships.* San Francisco, California: Jossey-Bass.

Moore, C. W. 2003. *The Mediation Process: Practical Strategies for Resolving Conflict.* San Francisco, California: Jossey-Bass.

Pritchard, Ray. 2005. *The Healing Power of Forgiveness.* Eugene, Oregon: Harvest House.

Rushnell, S. & DuArt, L. 2011. *Couples Who Pray: The Most Intimate Act Between a Man and a Woman.* Nashville, Tennessee: Thomas Nelson.

Simkins, W. E. & Fidandis. 1971. *Mediation and the Dynamics of Collective Bargaining.* Washington, DC: Bureau of National Affairs, Inc.

Ury, W. L. & Brett, J. M. 1988. *Getting Disputes Resolved: Designing Systems to Cut the Cost of Conflict.* San Francisco, California: Jossey-Bass.

If, after reading this book, you would like to work with Hezekiah Brown's professional services, please contact him either by telephone (252) 335-2439 or email—hez38@aol.com.

He offers services to individuals, businesses, churches, hospitals, and other organizations. This includes mediation and arbitration of disputes, guidance and help for individuals and businesses in dealing with conflict, training and consultation in conflict prevention, and employment discrimination mediation. Typical situations include marital, commercial, consumer, family, employee/employer, and landlord/tenant disputes. Both parties work together with the assistance of a mediator to achieve resolution.

CPSIA information can be obtained
at www.ICGtesting.com
Printed in the USA
JSHW031433220221
11892JS00001BA/4

9 781649 085221